CHILD PSYCHOLOGY

Understanding the foundations of
Child Psychology

Dr.Y. Narasimha Raja

Ph.D., MBA, M.Sc. Psychology
Asst. Professor –School of Management,
Presidency University, Bengaluru

Email: ynraja.phd@gmail.com
Web: www.ynraja.com

Dr.Y.Narasimha Raja

Copyrights Certification @ 2024

CHILD PSYCHOLOGY

MRP: Indian Rupees (INR) 220/-
Publishers: Notion Press
800, West EI Camino Real #180,California USA 94040

Devotional Dedication
to
Godess mother Saraswathi
Sri Sringeri Sharadamba

Dr.Y.Narasimha Raja

Index

Preface

"Children must be taught how to think, not what to think." —
Margaret

This book offers a comprehensive exploration of child psychology, covering essential aspects of children's development and well-being. Structured around key topics such as physical, cognitive, social, and moral growth, it provides insight into how children learn, communicate, and interact with their environment. *This book, is structured into the following topics:*

- ✓ Introduction to Child Psychology
- ✓ Developmental Stages of Childhood
- ✓ Physical Development in Children
- ✓ Cognitive Development in Children
- ✓ Socialization and Social Development
- ✓ Behavioral Development and Challenges
- ✓ Language & Communication Development
- ✓ Moral Development in Children
- ✓ Influence of Family and Culture
- ✓ The Role of Education in Child Psychology
- ✓ Child Mental Health and Well-being
- ✓ The Digital Age
- ✓ Gender Identity and Child Development
- ✓ Adolescence and Emotional Turmoil
- ✓ Childhood Disorders & Management
- ✓ Child Abuse & Neglect
- ✓ The Role of Play in Child Development
- ✓ Resilience and Coping in Childhood
- ✓ The Future of Child Psychology

This book is written in simple language, advised to consult the medical practioner for any issues.

With you and for you

Dr. Y. Narasimha Raja

Dr.Y.Narasimha Raja

About the Author

Dr. Y. Narasimha Raja multifaceted professional with significant contributions to the fields of Psychology, Management, and Human Resources. His extensive educational background, with a Ph.D. in Management Studies, and Master of Business Administration, Master of Science in Psychology and multiple master's degrees, complements his over 22 years of experience in corporate and academic sectors across India and internationally. As an award-winning HR practitioner and corporate trainer.

Book Publications
1. Highly Effective Parenting Skills
2. Highly Effective Teaching Skills
3. The best & smart Teaching techniques
4. Happy Parenting Skills
5. Stage Fear
6. Highly effective Public Speaking Skills
7. Phobias-Overview on 165 phobias
8. Neuro Disorders
9. Counseling Skills
10. How to change life better?
11. Positive Psychlogy for a Successful people.
12. Don't Overthink
13. The art of Winning Interviews
14. Group Discussion Techniques
15. Child Psychology

Chapter 1
Introduction to Child Psychology

Children are not things to be molded, but are people to be unfolded." — Jess Lair

Child psychology is the scientific study of children's mental, emotional, and social development from infancy through adolescence. It focuses on understanding how children grow, learn, and adapt to their environments. Child psychologists study the cognitive (thinking), behavioral, emotional, and social processes that shape a child's overall development.

In essence, child psychology seeks to understand not just how children change physically, but how they develop mentally and emotionally over time. It also looks at external influences, such as family, peers, and cultural factors, and their impact on a child's growth. Understanding child psychology helps caregivers and educators provide appropriate support at each stage of development.

Dr.Y.Narasimha Raja

The Importance of Understanding Child Development

"Children are like wet cement; whatever falls on them makes an impression." - Haim Ginott

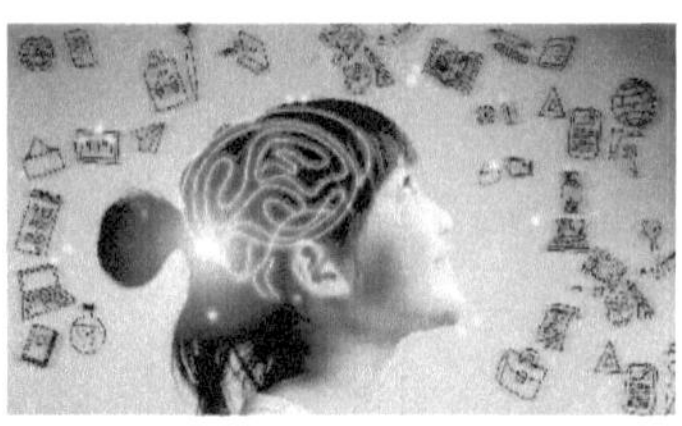

Understanding child development is crucial for helping children reach their full potential. Children undergo rapid changes during their early years, and their environment, experiences, and relationships play a significant role in shaping who they become. Knowledge of child psychology allows parents, teachers, and caregivers to create environments that foster healthy development.

Why Child Development is Important:

- **Emotional Well-being**: Children need emotionally secure environments to feel safe and thrive. Understanding emotional development helps caregivers respond to children's needs effectively.
- **Behavioral Guidance**: Knowledge of typical behaviors at different stages helps distinguish between normal developmental phases and potential behavioral problems.
- **Learning and Education**: Children learn in unique ways. Understanding how cognitive abilities develop ensures that children receive the right educational support at the right time.

2

- **Early Intervention**: Recognizing developmental delays or challenges early can lead to timely intervention, preventing long-term difficulties.

Example 1: Understanding Emotional Outbursts

A 3-year-old who throws tantrums may not be acting out of defiance but because they are unable to express their emotions verbally. Understanding that emotional regulation develops over time helps caregivers respond with patience and teach the child how to manage emotions.

Example 2: Promoting Healthy Relationships

Children who are socially engaged at a young age tend to develop stronger communication skills. For instance, a child who is encouraged to share and cooperate in preschool settings often has better peer relationships later in life.

Example 3: Identifying Learning Difficulties

Understanding child development helps detect learning difficulties early. For instance, a 7-year-old struggling with reading may benefit from an evaluation for dyslexia. Early diagnosis and tailored educational strategies improve learning outcomes.

According to the CDC (Centers for Disease Control and Prevention), about 1 in 6 children aged 3 to 17 years in the U.S. has a developmental disability, and early detection can significantly improve long-term outcomes.

Historical Perspectives and Key Theories in Child Psychology

"Every child is an artist. The problem is how to remain an artist once we grow up." - *Pablo Picasso*

The study of child psychology has evolved over time, with significant contributions from pioneering psychologists. These historical perspectives have shaped our understanding of how children grow and develop, leading to key theories that are still used today.

Key Historical Figures and Their Theories:

1. **Jean Piaget's Cognitive Development Theory**

Jean Piaget was one of the most influential figures in child psychology. He proposed that children pass through four stages of cognitive development: sensorimotor, preoperational, concrete operational, and formal operational. Each stage represents a different way of thinking and understanding the world.

Example 1: A toddler in the sensorimotor stage learns about the world through physical interaction, such as picking up and shaking toys to understand cause and effect.

Example 2: During the preoperational stage, a 5-year-old might engage in imaginative play, pretending a block is a car, illustrating symbolic thinking.

Example 3: A 9-year-old in the concrete operational stage develops logical thinking, understanding that water poured from one container to another still has the same volume (the concept of conservation).

Statistics: Research shows that Piaget's stages of cognitive development occur at roughly the same age across different cultures, though the speed of progress may vary depending on environmental factors (Barrouillet, 2015).

2. Sigmund Freud's Psychosexual Development Theory

Sigmund Freud introduced the concept that childhood experiences play a critical role in personality development. His theory emphasized that children go through various psychosexual stages that influence their behavior.

Example 1: In the oral stage (0-1 year), babies derive pleasure from sucking and feeding. A securely fed baby may grow up with a sense of comfort.

Example 2: During the anal stage (1-3 years), toddlers experience control over bodily functions, with successful toilet training contributing to a sense of independence.

Example 3: The phallic stage (3-6 years) involves the child becoming aware of their gender identity, often identifying with the same-sex parent.

Case Study: Freud's theory was tested in the "Little Hans" case study, where a child's fear of horses was linked to unresolved feelings about his father, providing early evidence of Freud's psychosexual stages.

3.   Erik Erikson's Psychosocial Development Theory

Erik Erikson expanded on Freud's ideas, proposing eight stages of psychosocial development that span across a person's life. His theory focuses on the social and emotional development of individuals, emphasizing that each stage involves a conflict that must be resolved.

Example 1: In the "trust vs. mistrust" stage (0-1 year), if a child's needs are consistently met, they develop trust in the world.

Example 2: During the "autonomy vs. shame and doubt" stage (1-3 years), toddlers who are encouraged to explore develop independence, while over-criticism may result in doubt

Example 3: In the "initiative vs. guilt" stage (3-6 years), children begin asserting control over their environment, developing initiative when encouraged to lead play activities.

Research Reference: A 2018 study by Simmons et al. confirmed that positive resolution of Erikson's early stages (trust, autonomy, and initiative) is correlated with better emotional outcomes in adolescence.

Developmental Stages of Childhood

"Childhood is the most beautiful of all life's seasons."
- Jerry Smith

Childhood development is commonly divided into distinct stages, each marked by specific emotional, cognitive, and social milestones. These stages allow for a structured understanding of a child's growth.

1. Infancy (0-2 years)

Infancy is a period of rapid physical, emotional, and cognitive development. Babies learn to trust caregivers, form emotional bonds, and begin exploring their environment.

Example 1: Emotional Attachment A securely attached baby, whose caregivers respond promptly to their needs, tends to be more confident as they explore their surroundings.

Example 2: Object Permanence Around 8-12 months, babies begin to understand that objects still exist even when out of sight. For instance, a baby searching for a toy hidden under a blanket shows they have achieved object permanence.

Example 3: Imitative Behavior A 1-year-old may start imitating their parents' actions, such as waving goodbye or clapping their hands. This early form of social learning is crucial for developing communication skills.

Statistics: According to UNICEF, over 80% of brain development occurs before the age of 3, emphasizing the importance of early childhood experiences in shaping future outcomes.

2. Early Childhood (2-6 years)

This stage is marked by the development of language, imagination, and social skills. Children learn through play and begin forming relationships outside the family unit.

Example 1: Language Explosion By age 3, most children experience a vocabulary explosion, allowing them to communicate their needs, thoughts, and emotions more effectively.

Example 2: Cooperative Play Around age 4, children engage in cooperative play, where they learn to share and take turns, developing essential social skills for peer interactions.

Example 3: Developing a Sense of Self At this stage, children start asserting independence, saying things like "I can do it myself." This reflects their growing sense of autonomy and self-awareness.

3. Middle Childhood (6-12 years)

During middle childhood, children gain a deeper understanding of the world around them. School becomes a central part of their lives, and they begin developing a sense of identity based on their achievements and peer relationships.

Example 1: Peer Relationships Children start forming close friendships, which help them understand loyalty, empathy, and social hierarchies.

Example 2: Academic Skills Children develop critical thinking and problem-solving skills through formal education. For instance, a child mastering multiplication tables or learning to write essays is building cognitive foundations for future learning.

Example 3: Self-Discipline By age 10, children begin to develop self-discipline, understanding the importance of following rules, completing homework, and taking responsibility for their actions.

Statistics: A report by the National Institute of Mental Health (2019) states that 1 in 5 children in middle childhood experience anxiety related to academic performance, indicating the pressure children may face during this stage.

4. Adolescence (12-18 years)

Adolescence is a time of significant physical, emotional, and social changes as children transition into adulthood. Identity formation, peer relationships, and independence become central themes.

Example 1: Identity Exploration Adolescents explore different aspects of their identity, including gender, sexuality, career aspirations, and personal values. They may experiment with different social groups or hobbies as part of this process.

Example 2: Peer Influence During adolescence, peer relationships become increasingly important. Teenagers may conform to peer group norms to gain acceptance, which can sometimes lead to risky behavior, such as experimenting with alcohol or tobacco.

Example 3: Emotional Regulation Adolescents learn to manage more complex emotions, such as romantic feelings, peer pressure, and academic stress. They may seek out coping mechanisms, like journaling or talking with friends, to process their emotions.

Research Reference: According to a study by Steinberg (2020), teenagers who have strong peer relationships and supportive family dynamics are more likely to navigate adolescence with fewer emotional and behavioral challenges.

Conclusion

Child psychology provides a comprehensive understanding of how children grow and develop. By examining historical perspectives, key theories, and the various stages of childhood, we can better appreciate the complexity of a child's emotional, social, and cognitive growth. This knowledge is invaluable for parents, educators, and mental health professionals in supporting children's well-being and development.

Chapter-2
Warning signs that Child Needs Help

Children go through many phases as they grow, and some behavioral, emotional, social, and physical changes are entirely natural. However, certain persistent patterns can signal underlying issues that may require additional support or intervention. This chapter explores specific warning signs across five primary categories—behavioral changes, emotional warning signs, social withdrawal and isolation, academic performance, and physical complaints and health.

These signs provide insight into a child's mental health and well-being and help caregivers, educators, and healthcare professionals identify when a child may need help.

1. Behavioral Changes

Behavioral shifts are often the most visible signs that a child may be struggling. Recognizing these changes can be essential in identifying the root causes of a child's distress and implementing appropriate support.

Sudden Outbursts of Anger : Unexplained anger can stem from frustration, stress, or an inability to express complex emotions. If a typically calm child suddenly begins having frequent angry outbursts, it may indicate they feel overwhelmed or misunderstood.

Frequent Tantrums or Displays of Extreme Frustration Tantrums are common in young children but should decrease as they age. Frequent or intense tantrums in older children can signal emotional distress or difficulty coping with frustration. It may suggest underlying anxiety, impulsivity, or unprocessed trauma.

Defiance or Oppositional Behavior That Is Out of Character: : When a child starts displaying defiant or oppositional behavior, it may indicate they're experiencing feelings of loss, insecurity, or a need for control in an environment that feels unpredictable. Such behavior can also arise from unmet needs for attention or connection.

Withdrawal from Previously Enjoyed Activities: Children withdrawing from hobbies they once loved may be a sign of depression or low self-esteem. A sudden lack of interest in enjoyable activities often correlates with feelings of apathy or sadness and can be an early indication of emotional challenges.

Constant Fidgeting or Inability to Sit Still : A child who suddenly becomes overly restless may be experiencing anxiety or could be struggling with attention issues. Inability to sit still can manifest in classroom settings, impacting academic performance and social interactions.

Increased Aggression, Such as Hitting or Shouting Aggressive behaviors, particularly if they're new or unusual for the child, often reflect underlying frustration or unresolved anger. Children may lack the tools to verbalize their feelings and instead act out physically or verbally.

Risk-Taking Behavior Unusual for Their Age : Engaging in risk-taking behaviors like running away or playing with dangerous objects can suggest the child is seeking stimulation or an escape from emotional pain. Such actions often indicate underlying issues with impulse control, peer pressure, or self-worth.

Self-Harm or Talk of Self-Injury : Self-harm is a critical warning sign of emotional distress, often linked to feelings of shame, anger, or a desire for control. It's essential to take any mention or sign of self-harm seriously and seek immediate support.

Excessive Crying or Tearfulness Without an Obvious Cause . Children who cry frequently and without clear reason may be struggling with unprocessed sadness, anxiety, or emotional overload. This behavior can suggest they are experiencing an emotional struggle they're unable to articulate.

Compulsive Behaviors : Compulsions like excessive handwashing, counting, or organizing objects may suggest underlying anxiety. These repetitive actions can provide a temporary sense of control, but excessive compulsive behaviors may indicate conditions like Obsessive-Compulsive Disorder (OCD).

2. **Emotional Warning Signs**

Emotional health significantly impacts a child's development, well-being, and relationships. Recognizing emotional warning signs can help adults support a child's mental health needs.

Persistent Sadness or Hopelessness *:* Long-lasting sadness or feelings of hopelessness are classic symptoms of depression. Persistent sadness often manifests as low energy, tearfulness, or a lack of enthusiasm for life.

Extreme Sensitivity to Rejection or Criticism *:* Children who are overly sensitive to criticism may have fragile self-esteem. This sensitivity can arise from experiences of failure, feelings of inadequacy, or difficulty in coping with mistakes.

Frequent Mood Swings *:* Mood swings, particularly if they're extreme or unpredictable, may indicate difficulty regulating emotions. While mood fluctuations are natural, intense changes in mood could suggest bipolar tendencies or hormonal imbalances.

Fearfulness or Expressions of Extreme Worry*:* Excessive worry or constant fear is often indicative of anxiety. Children may worry about school performance, family issues, or peer relationships and might express fear through avoidance, isolation, or physical complaints.

Expressions of Low Self-Worth: Statements like "I'm not good enough" reflect negative self-perception, often resulting from repeated failures, bullying, or emotional neglect. Low self-worth can lead to social withdrawal and decreased motivation.

Child Psychology

Frequent Feelings of Guilt or Shame: Unwarranted guilt or shame can indicate that a child feels they are inherently flawed or responsible for things beyond their control. This is often seen in children who experience parental conflict, bullying, or trauma.

Excessive Worry About Future Events or Daily Tasks

Children who excessively worry may have generalized anxiety. Worrying about future events, even routine ones, can prevent them from enjoying the present, impacting their development and overall well-being.

Fixation on Certain Thoughts or Fears : A child with a constant fear of failure or other repetitive thoughts may be struggling with anxiety or OCD. They may fixate on a specific thought pattern, disrupting their focus on other activities.

Talk of Feeling Unloved or Unworthy : Statements about feeling unloved can signal depression or low self-esteem. Children expressing these feelings often need reassurance, guidance, and emotional support from trusted adults.

Expressions of Feeling Overwhelmed by Small Tasks : Feeling overwhelmed by minor responsibilities can indicate stress, anxiety, or difficulty managing tasks. These children may need support in developing coping skills and setting realistic expectations.

3. Social Withdrawal and Isolation

Social withdrawal is a common sign of emotional distress and can affect a child's relationships, self-esteem, and development.

Avoiding Social Interactions : Children who avoid social interactions, especially if they previously enjoyed them, may be experiencing social anxiety, depression, or self-esteem issues.

Decline in Interest in Social Activities : A child's reduced interest in social activities may reflect emotional distress or difficulty with peer interactions, potentially indicating social anxiety or depression.

Spending More Time Alone : Choosing isolation over socializing can be a defense mechanism against feelings of inadequacy or anxiety, often signaling depression or withdrawal from potential stressors.

Frequent Arguments with Friends or Family : A sudden increase in arguments with loved ones may indicate unresolved frustration, poor emotional regulation, or underlying anger.

Refusal to Participate in School Activities Avoiding group activities or school events can indicate discomfort with social situations, often associated with social anxiety or feelings of inferiority.

Exclusion by Peers or Refusal to Interact : Peer exclusion can exacerbate feelings of loneliness and can occur when a child struggles to communicate effectively or has difficulty maintaining friendships.

Loss of Interest in Friendships : When a child stops engaging with friends they once valued, it may indicate sadness, low self-worth, or the onset of depression.

Difficulty Making or Keeping Friends : Challenges in forming or maintaining friendships can result from social anxiety, low self-confidence, or bullying experiences.

Bullying Others or Being Frequently Bullied : Both victims and perpetrators of bullying often struggle with low self-esteem and emotional regulation, and either behavior can be a sign of underlying stress or trauma.

Excessive Reliance on One Person for Comfort : Reliance on a single person for emotional support may suggest insecurity or attachment issues, and children with limited social networks often struggle to form healthy peer relationships.

4. Academic Performance

Academic struggles often mirror underlying psychological or emotional issues, providing insight into a child's well-being.

Sudden Drop in Grades : A decline in grades can indicate difficulty focusing, emotional distress, or a lack of motivation often related to mental health issues like anxiety or depression.

Frequent Complaints of Boredom or Disinterest in School : Constant complaints about boredom can signal attention deficits, disinterest due to external distractions, or a lack of engagement stemming from personal struggles.

Refusing to Complete Homework : Children who avoid homework might be feeling overwhelmed by tasks, lack confidence in their abilities, or experience feelings of inadequacy.

Difficulty Concentrating : Trouble focusing on schoolwork is often associated with anxiety, ADHD, or depression, all of which can impact cognitive functioning.

Frequent Absences from School : Regular school absences may indicate social anxiety, bullying, or a desire to escape stressors present in the school environment.

Forgetting Assignments or School Supplies : Consistently forgetting materials can reflect inattentiveness, anxiety, or organizational struggles, which may indicate ADHD or other cognitive issues.

Feelings of Academic Inadequacy : Statements like "I'm stupid" often indicate low self-confidence, feelings of inferiority, and may lead to avoiding schoolwork altogether.

Frequent Headaches or Stomachaches : Physical complaints that coincide with school days may be psychosomatic signs of anxiety, stress, or a desire to avoid specific social or academic situations.

Struggling to Understand Basic Concepts : Difficulty in understanding previously mastered subjects may signal a learning disability or cognitive regression related to emotional distress.

Frequent Detention or Disciplinary Issues : Disciplinary problems often reflect underlying behavioral or emotional issues, such as a lack of impulse control or defiance as a coping mechanism.

5. Physical Complaints and Health

Physical health often reflects a child's mental well-being, with physical complaints sometimes serving as indicators of emotional distress.

Frequent, Unexplained Physical Complaints: Unexplained complaints, like headaches or stomachaches, are common physical symptoms of anxiety or stress.

Changes in Eating Habits *:* Sudden changes in eating patterns can be linked to emotional states, such as stress-eating or loss of appetite due to depression.

Trouble Sleeping or Frequent Nightmares : Sleep disturbances are often signs of anxiety, trauma, or stress, impacting both physical and mental health.

Sudden Weight Loss or Gain : Unexpected weight changes can reflect emotional distress, altered eating habits, or underlying physical health concerns.

Fatigue or Low Energy Levels : Persistent fatigue, even with adequate rest, may suggest depression or an underlying medical condition that warrants attention.

Neglecting Personal Hygiene : Ignoring hygiene can signal depression or a lack of motivation, which is often connected to feelings of worthlessness or apathy.

Frequent Injuries or Accidents : A higher rate of injuries may reflect inattentiveness or impulsivity, often seen in children with ADHD or those experiencing stress.

Constant Complaints of Feeling Sick : Chronic complaints of illness may be psychosomatic, reflecting underlying anxiety, depression, or stress-related issues.

Frequent Skin Picking or Self-Soothing Behaviors : Repeated self-soothing actions can indicate anxiety or obsessive-compulsive tendencies, providing temporary relief from internal stress.

Unusual Body Odor Due to Poor Hygiene : Persistent poor hygiene is often an overlooked sign of depression or neglect, signaling that a child may not be receiving adequate support.

Conclusion

Identifying these signs is a crucial step in recognizing when a child might need extra help or support. While individual behaviors may not be concerning on their own, patterns of behavior across these categories can highlight underlying issues, guiding parents, caregivers, and professionals toward timely interventions.

Chapter-3
Developmental Stages of Childhood

"Children must be taught how to think, not what to think." – Margaret Mead

Childhood is a period of rapid growth and significant change. From birth through adolescence, children pass through various developmental stages, each characterized by physical, cognitive, emotional, and social milestones. Understanding these stages is crucial for parents, caregivers, educators, and psychologists as it provides a roadmap for what to expect and how to support children at each phase. Developmental stages of childhood give insight into how children evolve and gain new skills as they grow. These stages are interconnected and influenced by multiple factors, including genetics, environment, culture, and social interactions. By observing developmental milestones, we can ensure children are progressing healthily and address any potential delays or difficulties early on.

In this chapter, we will explore the **Developmental stages of childhood**,Focusing on

- **Infancy (birth to two years),**
- **Early childhood (two to six years),**
- **Middle childhood (six to twelve years) and**
- **Adolescence (twelve to eighteen years).**

We will provide three examples at each stage to illustrate developmental milestones, supported by relevant statistics and an action plan for fostering healthy development.

Overview of Developmental Milestones

Developmental milestones are specific abilities or skills that most children reach at certain ages. These include physical, cognitive, social, emotional, and communication skills. While every child develops at their own pace, these milestones act as checkpoints, helping caregivers identify typical growth patterns and any areas requiring attention.

Milestones are typically divided into:

- ❖ **Physical Development**: Includes gross and fine motor skills such as crawling, walking, and hand-eye coordination.
- ❖ **Cognitive Development**: Refers to how children learn, think, and solve problems.
- ❖ **Social and Emotional Development**: Involves children's ability to interact with others and manage their emotions.
- ❖ **Communication and Language Development**: Involves the ability to understand and use language.

1. Infancy: Birth to Two Years

Infancy is marked by the fastest rate of physical and brain growth in a person's life. During this stage, babies learn to trust their environment, bond with caregivers, and explore the world through their senses. Key developmental milestones in infancy include attachment, language acquisition, and motor skill development.

1.1. Examples of Developmental Milestones in Infancy

Example 1: Emotional Attachment

By six months, most babies show clear signs of attachment to their primary caregivers. This bond is demonstrated through behaviors like crying when the caregiver leaves the room and being comforted by their return. Secure attachment is crucial for healthy emotional development.

Example 2: Motor Skills Development

Around nine months, infants begin to crawl, allowing them to explore their environment independently. By twelve months, most babies take their first steps, marking a significant physical milestone. This motor development fosters independence and curiosity.

Example 3: Babbling and Early Language

By twelve months, babies typically begin to babble and form basic sounds like "mama" or "dada." Language development during this stage sets the foundation for more complex speech and communication in the coming years.

1.2. Statistics on Infant Development

- According to the **World Health Organization (WHO)**, around 90% of a child's brain develops by age five, with the most critical period being from birth to two years.

- **CDC data** reveals that approximately 65% of infants crawl by nine months, and 50% take their first steps by their first birthday.

2. Early Childhood: Two to Six Years

Early childhood is characterized by significant advances in cognitive, language, and social skills. Children develop their sense of self, engage in more complex play, and learn to regulate their emotions. This is a critical period for fostering curiosity, creativity, and social interaction.

2.1. Examples of Developmental Milestones in Early Childhood

Example 1: Language Explosion

By age three, most children experience a significant increase in their vocabulary, often referred to as the "language explosion." They can form sentences of three to four words, and by age four or five, they can communicate effectively with adults and peers.

Example 2: Imaginative Play

During this stage, children engage in imaginative play, which allows them to experiment with different roles and scenarios. A five-year-old might pretend to be a teacher, doctor, or superhero, demonstrating their understanding of the world around them.

Example 3: Emotional Self-Regulation

Children around age four begin to learn how to regulate

their emotions. For instance, instead of throwing tantrums when frustrated, a four-year-old might use words to express their feelings or seek help from an adult.

2.2. Statistics on Early Childhood Development

- Research from **Harvard's Center on the Developing Child** shows that 80% of children's language ability is established by the age of five.
- According to **UNICEF**, 90% of a child's brain architecture is formed by age five, highlighting the importance of early childhood for cognitive and emotional development.

3. Middle Childhood: Six to Twelve Years

Middle childhood is a period of steady growth, both physically and mentally. During this stage, children develop more refined motor skills, strengthen their academic abilities, and form stronger social connections. This stage is also when children develop a sense of independence and responsibility.

3.1. Examples of Developmental Milestones in Middle Childhood

Example 1: Peer Relationships

During middle childhood, friendships become more important and stable. Children begin to form relationships based on shared interests and values. A 10-year-old might have a close-knit group of friends and learn the importance of loyalty and compromise in these friendships.

Example 2: Academic Skills and Problem-Solving

Children in middle childhood improve their academic skills, such as reading, writing, and arithmetic. A nine-year-old may start reading chapter books independently and solving more complex math problems, which is indicative of cognitive growth.

Example 3: Developing Self-Esteem

At this stage, children's self-esteem is often tied to their abilities and achievements. A 10-year-old may feel proud of their accomplishments, such as winning a soccer game or receiving a good grade, which contributes to their sense of self-worth.

3.2. Statistics on Middle Childhood Development

- The **National Institute of Mental Health** (NIMH) reports that 80% of middle childhood is spent developing cognitive abilities, with reading and math skills improving significantly between ages six and twelve.
- **CDC statistics** indicate that nearly 90% of children can read and write proficiently by age twelve, highlighting the academic growth of this stage.

4. Adolescence: Twelve to Eighteen Years

Adolescence is a time of profound change, marked by physical growth, emotional fluctuations, and identity formation. During this stage, children transition from childhood into adulthood, facing challenges related to independence, peer pressure, and future planning.

4.1. *Examples of Developmental Milestones in Adolescence*

Example 1: Identity Exploration

During adolescence, teenagers begin to explore their identity, which includes developing personal values, beliefs, and career aspirations. A sixteen-year-old might question their future goals, experiment with different social groups, and seek to define who they are separate from their family.

Example 2: Peer Influence and Social Relationships

Adolescence is also a time when peer relationships and influence become paramount. A fifteen-year-old might prioritize friendships and seek validation from peers, sometimes leading to experimentation with new behaviors, both positive and negative.

Example 3: Emotional Regulation and Independence

By late adolescence, most teenagers are learning how to manage complex emotions, such as romantic feelings or academic stress. For instance, a seventeen-year-old might cope with the pressures of college applications by seeking advice from a trusted adult or practicing stress-relief strategies.

4.2. *Statistics on Adolescent Development*

- According to the **American Psychological Association (APA)**, approximately 85% of adolescents report feeling the influence of peer pressure during their teenage years, particularly related to social behaviors and decision-making.
- **WHO statistics** show that nearly 80% of adolescent identity formation occurs between ages

12 and 18, making this period critical for personal and social development.

Action Plans

1. Infancy (Birth to Two Years)

- **Action Plan**: Foster secure attachment by responding promptly to an infant's needs and creating a nurturing environment. Engage in sensory play to promote motor skills development.

2. Early Childhood (Two to Six Years)

- **Action Plan**: Encourage imaginative play and language development by reading to children and engaging in creative activities. Provide opportunities for children to interact with peers and practice sharing and emotional regulation.

3. Middle Childhood (Six to Twelve Years)

- **Action Plan**: Support academic growth by offering a structured learning environment and helping children develop problem-solving skills. Encourage peer interactions through group activities and sports to build social skills.

4. Adolescence (Twelve to Eighteen Years)

- **Action Plan**: Promote independence by allowing adolescents to make decisions while providing guidance. Encourage healthy peer relationships and help teenagers navigate challenges like peer pressure and identity exploration.

Conclusion

The developmental stages of childhood—from infancy through adolescence—are filled with milestones that shape a child's physical, cognitive, emotional, and social growth. Understanding these stages and the milestones that accompany them allows caregivers to provide the appropriate support and interventions at each phase of development. By fostering secure attachments, encouraging exploration and learning, and supporting independence, we can help children navigate these stages and grow into well-adjusted adults.

Chapter 4
Physical Development in Children

"Children are not just little adults. They think differently and are in constant stages of development."- **Jean Piaget**

Physical development is a crucial aspect of a child's overall growth, influencing their abilities to explore the world, engage in social interactions, and participate in learning activities. It includes changes in the size, shape, and functioning of a child's body and also encompasses the development of motor skills that allow children to interact with their environment. This chapter will explore key areas of physical development, including growth patterns, physical milestones, motor skill development, and the significant role that nutrition and health play in shaping physical growth.

Growth Patterns and Physical Milestones

Children's physical growth follows a relatively predictable sequence, although individual rates can vary. Understanding these patterns can help caregivers and educators track a child's development and identify any potential concerns.

1. **Prenatal and Infant Growth:**

From conception to birth, a child undergoes rapid physical changes. By the time a baby is born, their body has grown from a microscopic cell to a fully formed infant with functioning organs. This is the most rapid phase of growth in a human's life. Infants typically double their birth weight by five months and triple it by their first birthday. Height also increases significantly during this period.

2. Toddler Growth (Ages 1-3):

After the first year, growth begins to slow down, but it remains steady. Toddlers usually grow around 4 to 5 inches in height each year and gain about 5 pounds. Milestones during this period include walking independently, running, and improved hand-eye coordination. By age three, children have more control over their physical movements, such as throwing, catching, and riding tricycles.

3. Early Childhood (Ages 3-6):

Children in this age group typically grow 2 to 3 inches in height per year. Muscle mass and coordination also increase significantly during early childhood. This period is marked by improvements in balance, strength, and coordination. Children become more adept at running, jumping, and skipping. Fine motor skills also begin to sharpen, allowing them to perform more detailed tasks such as cutting with scissors or drawing recognizable shapes.

4. Middle Childhood (Ages 6-12):

Growth during middle childhood continues at a slower, steadier rate. Children typically grow about 2 inches per year and gain between 4 to 7 pounds annually. Physical milestones in this phase include refined motor skills and greater physical stamina. By this age, children can engage in more complex physical activities, such as organized sports or dance, which require strength, coordination, and endurance. Puberty marks the end of this phase, with rapid growth spurts for both boys and girls, typically starting around ages 10 to 12.

Motor Skill Development: Gross and Fine Motor Skills

Motor skill development is a key part of physical growth and involves the refinement of both gross and fine motor skills.

1. Gross Motor Skills:

Gross motor skills involve large body movements and the coordination of the core muscles in the arms, legs, and torso. These skills are crucial for basic movements such as sitting, walking, running, jumping, and maintaining balance.

Infancy and Early Toddler Years: During infancy, gross motor milestones include rolling over, sitting without support, crawling, and eventually walking. Toddlers quickly transition to running, climbing, and jumping by age two or three.

Preschool Years: As children grow, their balance, coordination, and strength improve. By the age of five, children typically have the physical control to engage in activities like riding a bike, skipping, and participating in more structured play or sports.

Middle Childhood: By the time children reach middle childhood, gross motor skills are refined enough to allow for more complex physical activities, such as playing soccer, swimming, or gymnastics.

2. Fine Motor Skills:

Fine motor skills involve more precise movements that require control over smaller muscles, especially in the hands and fingers. These skills are essential for tasks such as grasping objects, writing, and manipulating tools.

- ❖ **Infancy:** During infancy, fine motor development begins with reflexive movements like grasping. By around nine months, babies start to develop the pincer grasp, enabling them to pick up small objects between their thumb and forefinger.

- ❖ **Toddler and Preschool Years:** As children reach toddlerhood, they begin to refine these skills by using utensils, building with blocks, or turning pages in a book. By preschool, children can perform more intricate tasks, such as buttoning clothing, drawing, and beginning to write letters and numbers.

- ❖ **Middle Childhood:** Fine motor skills become highly developed in middle childhood, allowing children to engage in activities requiring precision and control, such as writing neatly, playing musical instruments, or engaging in detailed art projects.

Both gross and fine motor skills are essential for children's independence and their ability to interact with the world.

Impact of Nutrition and Health on Physical Growth

Nutrition and overall health are critical factors that directly influence a child's physical development. Adequate nutrition fuels growth, supports brain development, and ensures that children have the energy and vitality needed for their daily activities.

1. Importance of a Balanced Diet:

A balanced diet provides the necessary vitamins, minerals, and macronutrients (proteins, carbohydrates, and fats) that are essential for growth. Proper nutrition is particularly important during periods of rapid growth, such as infancy, early childhood, and adolescence.

- **Proteins** are essential for muscle growth and repair.
- **Calcium and Vitamin D** are vital for bone health, particularly during the growth spurts of childhood and adolescence.
- **Iron** is crucial for cognitive development and overall energy levels. Iron-deficiency anemia can lead to developmental delays and reduced physical stamina.
- **Healthy fats** support brain development, especially during the first few years of life when the brain grows rapidly.

2. Malnutrition and Its Effects:

Poor nutrition can significantly impair a child's physical development. Malnutrition can lead to stunted growth, weakened immune systems, delayed motor skill development, and cognitive deficits. Children who do not receive sufficient nutrition are at risk of experiencing delays in reaching physical milestones, which can affect their overall development and academic performance.

3. Role of Physical Health and Activity:

Regular physical activity is also essential for healthy growth. Exercise helps to strengthen muscles, improve coordination, and build stamina. Children who engage in regular physical activity are more likely to have strong bones, healthy muscles, and a lower risk of developing chronic health conditions such as obesity or type 2 diabetes. Physical activity is also important for motor skill development, as it provides opportunities for practice and refinement.

4. Impact of Health Conditions:

Chronic illnesses or conditions such as asthma, obesity, or developmental delays can impact physical development. These conditions may restrict a child's ability to engage in physical activities or affect their overall energy levels and nutritional needs. Access to healthcare and early intervention for any health concerns is critical to ensure children reach their full physical potential.

Conclusion

Physical development in children is a dynamic process shaped by genetic, environmental, and behavioral factors. While growth patterns and physical milestones provide general guidelines, each child's development is unique. Motor skill development, both gross and fine, enables children to explore their world and gain independence.

Dr.Y.Narasimha Raja

Chapter 5
Cognitive Development in Children

"The child is both a hope and a promise for mankind." Maria Montessori

Cognitive development in children is a critical aspect of their overall growth, shaping how they perceive, think, and understand the world around them. As children develop, they transition through various stages of thinking, problem-solving, memory, and language acquisition. These cognitive shifts are essential for success in school, relationships, and life. According to UNICEF, early childhood development lays the foundation for a child's future learning and well-being, with about 80% of a child's brain development occurring by age 3. Understanding the major theories of cognitive development and how children process information is crucial for parents, educators, and caregivers in supporting a child's intellectual growth.

Child Psychology

Cognitive development is influenced by various factors, including genetics, environment, and social interactions. Two of the most influential theorists in this area are Jean Piaget and Lev Vygotsky, who offered distinctive perspectives on how children learn and grow cognitively. In addition to these classical theories, modern understanding of cognitive growth incorporates insights from the information-processing model and emphasizes the pivotal role of play in fostering intellectual abilities.

Piaget's Stages of Cognitive Development

Jean Piaget, a Swiss psychologist, is renowned for his groundbreaking work on cognitive development. Piaget proposed that children move through four stages of cognitive development, each characterized by different ways of thinking and learning.

1. **Sensorimotor Stage (Birth to 2 years):** In the sensorimotor stage, infants learn about the world through their senses and motor activities. They gradually develop object permanence, understanding that objects continue to exist even when they are out of sight. Piaget believed this stage marked the foundation of logical thinking.

2. **Preoperational Stage (2 to 7 years):** During the preoperational stage, children start to use symbols, such as words and images, to represent objects. However, their thinking is still egocentric, meaning they have difficulty seeing things from perspectives other than their own. Children in this stage also engage in pretend play, but their reasoning remains intuitive and lacks logical structure.

3. **Concrete Operational Stage (7 to 11 years):** In the concrete operational stage, children begin to think

logically about concrete objects and events. They can perform operations like addition and subtraction and understand the concept of conservation—the idea that quantity remains the same even when its shape changes. However, their thinking is still grounded in tangible experiences, making abstract thinking difficult.

4. Formal Operational Stage (11 years and up): The final stage of Piaget's theory is the formal operational stage, where children develop the ability to think abstractly, reason logically, and draw conclusions from hypothetical situations. They can consider multiple perspectives and use deductive reasoning, enabling them to tackle complex problems.

"The principal goal of education in the schools should be creating men and women who are capable of doing new things, not simply repeating what other generations have done." — Jean Piaget

This quotation highlights Piaget's emphasis on fostering independent thinking and creativity in children. His theory suggests that understanding children's cognitive stages allows educators to tailor learning experiences to promote deeper thinking and problem-solving skills.

Vygotsky's Theory of Social Development

Lev Vygotsky, a Russian psychologist, proposed a different approach to cognitive development, emphasizing the role of social interaction and culture. According to Vygotsky, cognitive development is inherently a social process, where learning occurs through interactions with more knowledgeable others, such as parents, teachers, or peers.

Child Psychology

1. The Zone of Proximal Development (ZPD):

One of Vygotsky's key concepts is the Zone of Proximal Development, which refers to the range of tasks a child can complete with the help of someone more knowledgeable. The ZPD represents the gap between what a child can do independently and what they can achieve with guidance. Vygotsky argued that cognitive development is most effective when children work within their ZPD, receiving support that challenges but does not overwhelm them.

2. Scaffolding:

Scaffolding is the process of providing children with temporary support or guidance until they can perform a task on their own. Teachers and caregivers scaffold by offering hints, encouragement, or modeling problem-solving strategies, gradually reducing assistance as the child becomes more competent.

4. Language and Thought:

Vygotsky also emphasized the importance of language in cognitive development. He believed that language is a powerful tool for thinking and problem-solving. As children engage in conversations with others, they internalize language, which shapes their thinking processes.

> "What a child can do in cooperation today, he can do alone tomorrow." — Lev Vygotsky

Vygotsky's theory underscores the social nature of learning, emphasizing that through collaboration, children can extend their cognitive abilities beyond what they can achieve independently. His work is foundational in understanding the importance of social environments in education.

Dr.Y.Narasimha Raja

Information Processing in Childhood

The information-processing model compares the human mind to a computer, suggesting that cognitive development is a continuous process in which children gradually improve their abilities to process information.

1. Attention and Memory:

Young children have limited attention spans and memory capacity, but these skills improve with age. As children grow, they become better at focusing on tasks, filtering out distractions, and retaining information. Strategies like rehearsal, chunking, and mnemonic devices are cognitive tools that enhance memory.

2. Executive Function:

Executive functions refer to higher-order cognitive skills such as planning, problem-solving, and self-control. These abilities are crucial for regulating behavior and achieving goals. Executive functions develop throughout childhood, with significant progress occurring in the preschool years and continuing into adolescence.

3. Processing Speed:

Another key aspect of cognitive development is processing speed, or the pace at which children take in and respond to information. As neural connections in the brain strengthen, children can process information more quickly, allowing them to complete tasks more efficiently.

"

This highlights the gradual refinement of cognitive processes in children. As they develop, children don't just accumulate knowledge; they become more efficient thinkers, capable of processing and integrating complex information.

The Role of Play in Cognitive Growth

Play is an essential part of childhood and is deeply intertwined with cognitive development. Through play, children explore the world, test out new ideas, and develop problem-solving skills.

1. Symbolic Play:

Symbolic play, such as pretending to be a teacher or playing house, helps children develop abstract thinking. By imagining scenarios and role-playing, children practice using symbols, enhancing their ability to think beyond the concrete and present.

2. Problem-Solving through Play:

Play often involves challenges that require problem-solving, such as building a tower of blocks or figuring out the rules of a game. These experiences help children learn to plan, experiment with different strategies, and adapt when things don't go as expected.

5. Social Play and Cognitive Skills:

Social play, such as playing games with others, also contributes to cognitive development by requiring children to negotiate rules, cooperate with peers, and take turns. These interactions help children develop theory of mind, which is the ability to understand that others have thoughts and perspectives different from their own.

"Play is the highest form of research." — *Albert Einstein*

Action Plans to Overcome Cognitive Developmental Challenges

Cognitive developmental challenges, such as delays in language, attention, or executive functioning, can be addressed through targeted interventions:

1. **Early Identification and Support:**

   Regular developmental screenings can identify cognitive delays early, allowing for timely intervention. Specialized learning programs, speech therapy, and behavioral interventions can help address specific challenges.

2. **Parental Involvement:**

   Parents play a key role in supporting cognitive growth. Engaging in activities like reading, playing educational games, and having conversations fosters a rich environment for cognitive development.

3. **Educational Strategies:**

   Teachers can use scaffolding, differentiated instruction, and hands-on learning experiences to cater to diverse learning needs. Structured environments that encourage exploration and inquiry are beneficial.

4. **Encouraging Play and Social Interaction:**

Providing opportunities for imaginative play and peer interaction helps children develop problem-solving skills and fosters cognitive and social development.

Conclusion

Cognitive development is a multifaceted process influenced by biological, environmental, and social factors. The theories of Piaget and Vygotsky provide foundational insights into how children think, learn, and grow. Modern research, including information-processing models, has further expanded our understanding of cognitive development, emphasizing the importance of attention, memory, and executive function.

Play remains a powerful tool for fostering cognitive growth, offering children the opportunity to explore, imagine, and learn through active engagement with their surroundings. By understanding the complexities of cognitive development, caregivers, educators, and policymakers can create environments that support optimal intellectual growth in children.

Fostering cognitive development is not only about addressing challenges but also about celebrating and nurturing the natural curiosity that drives children to learn and explore their world. Through intentional support and enriched experiences, children can reach their fullest cognitive potential.

Chapter-6
Socialization and Social Development

"The best way to make children good is to make them happy." Oscar Wilde

Socialization is the lifelong process through which individuals acquire the values, beliefs, and behaviors necessary to function effectively in society. For children, socialization is a crucial aspect of their overall development, shaping not only their behavior but also their identity and understanding of societal norms. Social development involves the gradual learning of skills that help individuals interact with others, form relationships, and navigate social environments. Research indicates that social interactions begin in infancy and continue to evolve throughout childhood and adolescence, deeply influencing an individual's emotional well-being and mental health. According to studies conducted by the American Academy of Pediatrics, early social experiences significantly impact a child's ability to form secure attachments and positive relationships later in life.

Early Social Interactions: Family, Friends, and Peers

Social development begins within the context of the family, as it is the primary socializing agent during the early years of a child's life. Family interactions lay the foundation for emotional security, communication skills, and the ability to form trusting relationships.

- ❖ **The Role of Family:** From birth, infants rely on their parents and caregivers to meet their basic needs, but family also plays an essential role in emotional and social development. Positive early interactions with caregivers, such as responsive parenting, promote secure attachment, which is crucial for the development of social and emotional regulation skills. Securely attached children tend to exhibit higher levels of social competence and better interpersonal relationships as they grow.

- ❖ **Friendships in Early Childhood:**As children grow and begin to engage with others outside the family, friendships become important. Friendships in early childhood are based on proximity and shared activities. These relationships help children learn social norms, such as taking turns, sharing, and empathy. Studies show that early friendships can enhance self-esteem and provide a foundation for more complex social interactions.

- ❖ **Peer Relationships:**While family relationships are crucial, peers become increasingly important as children move through childhood. Peer relationships are a primary context for learning social rules and negotiating conflicts.

Dr.Y.Narasimha Raja

Peer Relationships in Childhood

Peer relationships take on heightened importance during middle childhood, as children begin to spend more time outside the family unit, particularly in educational settings. These relationships significantly influence a child's self-concept, social skills, and emotional health.

❖ **The Importance of Peer Interactions:** During childhood, peer relationships provide a unique context for the development of social competence. Unlike family relationships, peer interactions involve individuals of similar age and status, which allows children to practice negotiation, cooperation, and conflict resolution. Studies suggest that children with strong peer relationships tend to have better emotional well-being and perform better academically.

❖ **Social Skills and Peer Acceptance:** Social skills such as sharing, empathy, and problem-solving are critical in gaining peer acceptance. Children who are able to engage in positive, prosocial behaviors are more likely to be accepted by their peers, while those who struggle with social interactions may experience rejection or bullying. Peer rejection during childhood is linked to emotional difficulties such as anxiety and depression.

❖ **The Role of Peer Groups:** As children age, peer groups begin to exert a stronger influence on behavior and identity. Peer groups offer a sense of belonging and provide a context for the development of norms and values outside of the family. Group membership can reinforce positive behaviors, such as cooperation and teamwork, but can also introduce negative influences, including peer pressure to engage in risky behaviors.

The Role of Schools in Socialization

Schools are among the most important institutions responsible for the socialization of children. In addition to their academic function, schools play a crucial role in fostering social skills, shaping behavior, and teaching societal norms and values.

❖ **Socialization through Education:** Schools are structured environments where children learn to interact with authority figures (teachers) and peers in a formal setting. The routine, rules, and expectations in schools teach children discipline, responsibility, and respect for authority. Moreover, schools encourage cooperative learning, where children work in groups, learning to collaborate, resolve conflicts, and share knowledge.

❖ **The Hidden Curriculum:** Beyond academic learning, schools impart what is known as the "hidden curriculum." This includes the transmission of cultural norms, values, and behaviors that are not explicitly taught but are ingrained through the social environment of the school. For example, schools often reinforce concepts such as punctuality, hard work, and competition, which are essential for functioning in adult society.

❖ **Extracurricular Activities and Social Development:** Participation in extracurricular activities, such as sports, music, or debate teams, provides additional opportunities for social development. These activities foster teamwork, leadership, and a sense of belonging, helping children develop confidence and social competence.

Adolescence and Identity Formation

Adolescence is a period of significant change, both physically and socially. During this time, individuals grapple with questions of identity, autonomy, and their role in society.

- ❖ **Identity Exploration:** Erik Erikson, a renowned developmental psychologist, identified the primary challenge of adolescence as "identity vs. role confusion." During this stage, adolescents explore various aspects of their identity, including gender roles, career aspirations, and personal beliefs. Peer relationships play a critical role in this process, as adolescents seek validation and understanding from their social group.

- ❖ **The Influence of Peer Groups in Adolescence:** As adolescents strive for independence, they often turn to peer groups for support and guidance. Friendships during adolescence become more intimate and emotionally significant, providing a sense of security and belonging. However, peer pressure can also be more intense during this period, influencing decisions related to risk-taking behaviors, such as experimenting with alcohol, drugs, or defying authority.

- ❖ **The Role of Media and Society:** In today's digital age, social media also plays a pivotal role in shaping adolescent identity. Exposure to diverse perspectives and cultures, as well as the pressures of social comparison, can significantly influence self-esteem and social behavior.

Action Plans to Overcome Socialization Challenges

Children and adolescents can face challenges in socialization, such as social anxiety, peer rejection, or difficulties in identity formation. Addressing these challenges requires targeted strategies:

Fostering Emotional Intelligence: Teaching children and adolescents how to recognize, understand, and manage their emotions can improve social interactions and relationships. Programs that promote emotional literacy can help children navigate social challenges with greater resilience.

Parental and Teacher Involvement: Supportive relationships with adults are critical for healthy social development. Parents and teachers can model positive social behavior, provide guidance on navigating peer relationships, and create environments that encourage cooperation and mutual respect.

Inclusive School Environments: Schools should focus on creating inclusive environments that celebrate diversity and promote acceptance. Anti-bullying programs, peer mentoring, and cooperative learning activities can help foster positive social interactions among students.

Encouraging Healthy Peer Relationships: Facilitating opportunities for children and adolescents to engage in positive peer relationships, such as through extracurricular activities or social clubs, can promote social development and reduce the risk of negative peer influences.

Conclusion

Socialization is a complex and ongoing process that begins in infancy and continues throughout life. Early social interactions with family and peers lay the foundation for later social skills, while schools play a significant role in shaping social behaviors and norms. Peer relationships are crucial during childhood and adolescence, influencing self-esteem, identity formation, and emotional well-being. Adolescence is a particularly critical period for identity exploration, where young individuals negotiate their place within society and form their unique sense of self.

By understanding the stages and agents of socialization, parents, educators, and society at large can support children and adolescents in developing the skills they need to form healthy relationships, navigate social environments, and build a strong sense of identity.

Chapter 7
Behavioral Development and Challenges

"Children are not things to be molded, but are people to be unfolded." — Jess Lair

The children's behaviors should be understood as part of their individual developmental journeys, rather than solely something to be controlled or corrected. Behavioral development is an integral aspect of a child's overall growth, influencing how they interact with their environment, parents, peers, and society at large. From the early years, children exhibit patterns of behavior that can reflect their cognitive, emotional, and social development. While some behaviors are part of the normal developmental process, others can be signs of behavioral challenges that may need intervention. According to the World Health Organization (WHO), 10-20% of children and adolescents globally experience mental health disorders, with behavioral challenges often forming a significant portion of these issues.

Understanding Common Behavioral Patterns in Children

Children's behaviors vary greatly depending on age, developmental stage, and environmental influences. Some behaviors are expected as part of normal development, while others may indicate underlying challenges.

Early Childhood Behavior Patterns: In early childhood, it is common for children to exhibit behaviors such as temper tantrums, defiance, and difficulty sharing. These behaviors often stem from a developing sense of autonomy and frustration with their limited communication skills. Between the ages of two and four, children are learning to assert independence, which can manifest as defiant or oppositional behaviors. According to the American Academy of Pediatrics, around 50-80% of toddlers will experience temper tantrums at some point.

School-Age Behavior Patterns: As children enter school, they begin to navigate complex social dynamics, which can influence their behavior. Peer relationships become more prominent, and behaviors such as competitiveness, social withdrawal, or bullying may emerge. School-aged children may also struggle with following rules or paying attention in structured environments like classrooms, which can sometimes be misinterpreted as behavioral problems when, in reality, they are still developing self-regulation and social skills.

Behavioral Disorders: ADHD, ODD, and Conduct Disorders

While some behavioral patterns are a normal part of growing up, others may signal more serious challenges, such as Attention Deficit Hyperactivity Disorder (ADHD), Oppositional Defiant Disorder (ODD), or Conduct Disorders. These disorders require careful attention, early diagnosis, and intervention to help children thrive in their personal, academic, and social lives.

ADHD (Attention Deficit Hyperactivity Disorder): ADHD is one of the most common neurodevelopmental disorders in children, affecting approximately 5-7% of children globally, according to the Centers for Disease Control and Prevention (CDC). Children with ADHD may exhibit symptoms such as difficulty concentrating, impulsivity, and hyperactivity. These behaviors can interfere with academic performance and social relationships. While the exact cause of ADHD remains unknown, research suggests a combination of genetic, environmental, and neurological factors.

ODD (Oppositional Defiant Disorder): Oppositional Defiant Disorder is characterized by a persistent pattern of angry, irritable, or defiant behavior toward authority figures. Children with ODD may frequently argue with adults, refuse to follow rules, or intentionally annoy others. A study by the American Psychological Association (APA) indicates that around 3-5% of children exhibit ODD behaviors, often beginning in early childhood. Without proper intervention, ODD can lead to more severe behavioral issues, such as Conduct Disorder.

Conduct Disorder: Conduct Disorder involves more serious behavioral problems, such as aggression, destruction of property, or violation of social norms and rules. Children with Conduct Disorder may engage in bullying, theft, or physical violence. This disorder is relatively rare compared to ADHD and ODD, but it poses significant challenges for both the child and their environment. Children with untreated Conduct Disorder are at higher risk of legal issues and difficulty in adulthood.

"The way we talk to our children becomes their inner voice." — Peggy O'Mara

This quote highlights the role of communication in shaping children's behavior. Understanding and addressing behavioral disorders requires careful, compassionate interaction that reinforces positive behavior and emotional regulation.

Parenting Styles and Their Impact on Behavior

Parenting styles play a significant role in shaping children's behaviors and their ability to manage emotions. Different parenting approaches can either mitigate or exacerbate behavioral challenges.

Authoritative Parenting: Authoritative parents balance warmth and responsiveness with clear expectations and boundaries. Studies show that children raised in authoritative households tend to exhibit better self-regulation, social competence, and lower rates of behavioral problems. These parents are supportive but firm, encouraging independence while maintaining control.

Authoritarian Parenting: Authoritarian parents are highly controlling and demand obedience, often with little warmth or flexibility. This strict approach can lead to children exhibiting either passive or rebellious behaviors. Children raised in authoritarian environments may struggle with self-esteem and become dependent on external validation, increasing the likelihood of behavioral issues such as aggression or social withdrawal.

Permissive Parenting: Permissive parents are lenient and indulgent, often avoiding confrontation or setting clear boundaries. While these parents may be nurturing, a lack of structure can result in children struggling to understand social rules and self-control. According to research published in the Journal of Child and Family Studies, children raised in permissive households are more prone to behavioral problems, such as impulsivity and difficulty adhering to social norms.

"Your children need your presence more than your presents." — Jesse Jackson

Managing Challenging Behaviors in Children

Managing challenging behaviors in children requires a multifaceted approach that includes both behavioral strategies and emotional support. Effective management not only addresses the behavior but also fosters a child's ability to self-regulate and develop healthy coping mechanisms.

Positive Reinforcement: One of the most effective strategies for managing challenging behaviors is positive reinforcement, where desired behaviors are rewarded to encourage their repetition. Instead of focusing on punishment for bad behavior, rewarding good behavior with praise, tokens, or privileges can significantly improve a child's behavior over time. For example, a child who successfully completes homework without distraction could be rewarded with extra playtime.

Consistent Routines and Boundaries: Children, especially those with behavioral challenges, benefit from consistent routines and clear expectations. Establishing daily routines for tasks like homework, chores, and bedtime can help children understand what is expected of them and reduce anxiety or defiance. Clear boundaries, when enforced consistently, help children feel secure and understood.

Emotional Coaching: Children with behavioral challenges often struggle with managing their emotions. Emotional coaching involves helping children recognize and label their emotions, followed by teaching them appropriate ways to express these feelings. For instance, when a child feels angry, a parent or caregiver can help them articulate their emotions rather than acting out physically. This method encourages emotional intelligence and better behavior over time.

4. Seeking Professional Support: For children with severe behavioral challenges, professional support may be necessary. Behavioral therapy, counseling, or cognitive-behavioral therapy (CBT) can help children develop skills to manage their behaviors. Parent training programs, where parents are taught strategies to manage disruptive behaviors effectively, have also proven effective.

"The most important thing that parents can teach their children is how to get along without them." — Frank A.

Action Plans to Overcome Behavioral Challenges

Early Identification and Diagnosis: Early screening for behavioral disorders such as ADHD and ODD is critical. Schools, pediatricians, and parents should work together to recognize early warning signs and seek timely professional assessments to initiate appropriate interventions.

Parenting Workshops and Resources: Offering parenting workshops that educate caregivers on different parenting styles, behavioral management techniques, and the importance of emotional support can have a significant impact. Programs should also include strategies for managing stress and building a strong parent-child bond.

School-Based Behavioral Support Programs: Schools can implement behavior management programs that promote positive behaviors, such as peer mentorship, behavioral contracts, and reward systems. Training teachers to recognize and manage challenging behaviors in the classroom is also essential.

Conclusion : Behavioral development is a critical component of a child's overall growth, and while some behaviors are part of normal development, others may require careful attention and intervention. Understanding common behavioral patterns, recognizing behavioral disorders, and the role of parenting styles provide valuable insights into managing challenging behaviors. With the right strategies—positive reinforcement, clear boundaries, and emotional coaching—alongside professional interventions when necessary, parents and caregivers can help children develop healthy behavioral habits.

Chapter 8
Language & Communication Development

"Language is the dress of thought." — Samuel

Language and communication skills are among the most important developmental milestones in a child's early years. They are essential for expressing needs, forming relationships, learning, and interacting with the environment. The process of language acquisition begins at birth and continues through early childhood, with each phase marked by distinct linguistic and communicative abilities. According to the World Health Organization (WHO), approximately 7-8% of children worldwide experience language or communication disorders, making it critical to understand language milestones, the theories behind language development, and ways to encourage language growth.

Language Milestones: From Babbling to Sentences

Babbling (4-6 months): Around 4-6 months, babies begin to experiment with sounds through babbling. This stage is characterized by repetitive consonant-vowel combinations like "ba-ba" or "da-da." While these sounds may not have meaning initially, they lay the foundation for future speech. Babbling also helps babies practice the physical act of speaking by moving their lips, tongue, and vocal cords.

First Words (12-18 months): By the age of one, most children utter their first words, which are often simple and related to their immediate environment, such as "mama," "dada," or "milk." These words carry meaning and are used intentionally to communicate needs or attract attention. A child's vocabulary typically grows rapidly during this phase, expanding from a few words to about 50-100 words by 18 months.

Two-Word Sentences (18-24 months): Between 18 and 24 months, children begin combining words to form simple two-word sentences, such as "more juice" or "big truck." This phase is known as "telegraphic speech," as children use only essential words to convey meaning, much like a telegram. Grammar starts to emerge at this stage, though it remains rudimentary.

Complex Sentences (3-4 years): By the age of three, children typically form more complex sentences and begin to grasp basic grammar rules. They can use plurals, past tense, and pronouns with greater accuracy. Their vocabulary also expands significantly, often reaching over 1,000 words by age four. This stage marks the beginning of more nuanced communication, including the ability to ask questions, describe events, and share ideas.

Dr.Y.Narasimha Raja

Theories of Language Development

Noam Chomsky's Nativist Theory: Chomsky is best known for his theory of Universal Grammar, which argues that humans are born with an innate ability to learn language. According to Chomsky, all children have a "language acquisition device" (LAD) that enables them to rapidly acquire the rules of language through minimal input. He believed that exposure to language triggers this inherent ability, allowing children to understand and produce complex sentences relatively quickly. Chomsky's theory highlights the biological foundation of language acquisition.

B.F. Skinner's Behaviorist Theory: In contrast to Chomsky, Skinner proposed that language is learned through operant conditioning. According to Skinner, children acquire language by imitating the speech of those around them and receiving reinforcement for correct usage. For instance, a child may learn to say "milk" because when they do, they are given milk. Skinner's theory emphasizes the role of the environment and reinforcement in language learning.

Lev Vygotsky's Social Interactionist Theory: Vygotsky argued that language development is a social process and is closely linked to cognitive development. He believed that children learn language through interaction with more knowledgeable others, such as parents, caregivers, or peers. According to Vygotsky, the Zone of Proximal Development (ZPD) is crucial for language acquisition, as children need guidance and support to reach their full linguistic potential. His theory emphasizes the importance of social context and communication in language development.

"Language shapes the way we think, and determines what we can think about." — Benjamin Lee Whorf

Communication Disorders in Childhood

While most children follow a typical path of language development, some may experience communication disorders that hinder their ability to express themselves or understand others.

Speech and Language Delays: Speech delays refer to a child's difficulty in producing sounds, while language delays involve challenges in understanding or using words. According to the American Speech-Language-Hearing Association (ASHA), speech and language delays affect around 10% of preschool-aged children. These delays can result from a variety of factors, including hearing impairments, developmental disorders, or environmental influences.

Autism Spectrum Disorder (ASD): Children with Autism Spectrum Disorder often exhibit difficulties in communication, both verbal and non-verbal. They may struggle with understanding social cues, maintaining conversations, or using language in a socially appropriate way. Approximately 1 in 54 children are diagnosed with ASD, according to the Centers for Disease Control and Prevention (CDC), and early intervention is crucial for improving language and communication outcomes.

Specific Language Impairment (SLI): Specific Language Impairment is a condition where a child has difficulty with language acquisition despite normal cognitive abilities. Children with SLI may have trouble forming sentences, using grammar correctly, or expanding their vocabulary. Studies suggest that SLI affects 7-8% of children entering school, and it can significantly impact academic performance and social interactions.

Dr. Y. Narasimha Raja

Encouraging Language Growth through Interaction

The role of interaction in language development cannot be overstated. Children learn language best through meaningful engagement with caregivers, peers, and their environment.

Talking and Reading: Talking to children regularly, even in infancy, helps stimulate their language development. Studies show that the amount of language a child hears during their early years is directly related to their vocabulary growth and language skills. Reading aloud to children from an early age also promotes literacy and exposes them to new words, sentence structures, and ideas.

Responsive Interaction: Children thrive when adults engage in responsive interaction, meaning they acknowledge and build on the child's communication attempts. For example, if a toddler says "dog," the caregiver might respond with, "Yes, that's a big dog!" This encourages the child to continue practicing language and expands their vocabulary.

Play-Based Learning: Play provides a natural context for language learning. Through imaginative play, children practice using language to express themselves, negotiate roles, and solve problems. Encouraging children to engage in role-playing, storytelling, and other language-rich activities fosters linguistic and social development.

"Play is the work of the child." — Maria Montessori

Action Plans to Overcome Language and Communication Challenges

Early Identification and Intervention: Regular developmental screenings can help identify language delays or communication disorders early. The sooner these issues are addressed, the better the long-term outcomes for the child. Speech therapy, language enrichment programs, and specialized interventions can significantly improve communication skills.

Parental Involvement: Parents play a key role in fostering language development. By talking, reading, and playing with their children, parents can create a language-rich environment that supports growth. Parental training programs can also equip caregivers with strategies to encourage communication in children with delays or disorders.

Inclusive Educational Environments: Schools and early childhood programs should provide inclusive environments where children with communication disorders can thrive. Teachers trained in language development and special education can tailor their instruction to meet the needs of all learners.

Use of Technology: Assistive technologies, such as speech-generating devices or apps that promote language learning, can support children with communication challenges. These tools can be especially helpful for children with Autism Spectrum Disorder or speech impairments, offering alternative ways to communicate.

Conclusion

Language and communication development are foundational for a child's cognitive, emotional, and social growth. Understanding the typical milestones of language acquisition, recognizing the theories that explain how children learn language, and addressing communication disorders through early intervention are essential steps in supporting every child's linguistic journey. Encouraging language growth through interaction—whether through talking, reading, or play—ensures that children have the tools they need to express themselves and connect with the world around them.

By fostering a supportive, language-rich environment at home and in educational settings, caregivers and educators can help children overcome communication challenges and reach their full potential in language development.

Chapter 9
Moral Development in Children

Moral development is a crucial aspect of childhood growth that reflects how children learn to differentiate between right and wrong, develop a sense of fairness, and cultivate ethical values. It involves the gradual development of a moral compass that helps children make decisions, interact with others, and integrate into society. Understanding the processes through which children develop morally can provide insight into their behavior, interactions, and decision-making. According to research by the American Psychological Association (APA), moral development begins in early childhood and continues throughout adolescence, with significant variations based on cultural, familial, and environmental influences.

Kohlberg's Stages of Moral Development

Lawrence Kohlberg, an influential American psychologist, expanded on the work of Jean Piaget to develop a comprehensive theory of moral development. His model is based on how individuals progress through different stages of moral reasoning, beginning in childhood and potentially continuing into adulthood. Kohlberg's theory is structured into three levels, each comprising two stages.

1. **Pre-Conventional Level (Early Childhood):**

At the pre-conventional level, moral reasoning is driven by external consequences. Children make decisions based on the desire to avoid punishment or gain rewards. In Stage 1, the "obedience and punishment" stage, children believe that rules set by authority figures must be followed to avoid punishment. In Stage 2, the "individualism and exchange" stage, moral reasoning is based on self-interest, and children start recognizing that different individuals have varying viewpoints.

2. Conventional Level (Middle Childhood to Adolescence):

During this level, children's moral reasoning shifts from self-interest to a focus on social relationships and the expectations of society. In Stage 3, the "good interpersonal relationships" stage, children make decisions based on seeking approval and maintaining relationships. In Stage 4, the "maintaining social order" stage, moral reasoning is guided by the belief that laws and social rules exist to maintain order and should be respected to avoid societal chaos.

3. Post-Conventional Level (Adolescence to Adulthood):

At this level, moral reasoning becomes more abstract, and individuals may start to question societal norms and laws. In Stage 5, the "social contract and individual rights" stage, individuals understand that laws are necessary but recognize that some may be unjust and can be changed. In Stage 6, the "universal ethical principles" stage, individuals follow self-chosen ethical principles, such as justice and equality, even if they conflict with laws or social rules.

"The moral development of a child is not the teaching of facts, but the awakening of conscience." — Johann

Piaget's Theory of Moral Reasoning

Jean Piaget, a pioneering developmental psychologist, also explored the evolution of moral reasoning in children. He identified two stages of moral reasoning that correspond to children's cognitive development.

1. Heteronomous Morality (Ages 4-7):

In the early stage, Piaget termed this the "morality of constraint." Children view rules as fixed and unchangeable, handed down by authority figures such as parents or teachers. They believe that consequences, rather than intentions, determine whether an action is right or wrong. For example, a child might think breaking two cups accidentally is worse than breaking one cup intentionally because the outcome (two broken cups) seems more significant.

2. Autonomous Morality (Ages 8+):

As children grow older and engage in more social interactions, they enter the "morality of cooperation." They begin to understand that rules are created by people and can be modified through mutual agreement. At this stage, children start valuing fairness, equality, and the intentions behind actions. They recognize that it's not just the outcome that matters but also why someone acted a certain way.

Piaget's theory highlights the shift from rigid thinking to a more flexible understanding of morality, as children learn that rules and ethics are not always black and white but can be negotiated and applied according to context.

"To understand is to forgive, even oneself." — Alexander

The Development of Ethics and Fairness in Children

Children's understanding of fairness and ethics is closely linked to their cognitive and emotional development. Even at a young age, children show signs of ethical reasoning, although it may be simplistic and focused on fairness in terms of equality.

1. Early Concepts of Fairness (Ages 2-5):

Research shows that even toddlers understand basic concepts of fairness, such as the idea that resources should be shared equally. A 2019 study published in Developmental Psychology found that children as young as three years old prefer equal distribution of rewards and become upset when they perceive inequality, even when it doesn't directly affect them.

2. Developing Empathy and Moral Reasoning (Ages 6-10):

As children grow, their understanding of fairness becomes more nuanced. They begin to recognize that equality is not always synonymous with fairness, and sometimes different people have different needs. For example, older children may understand that a younger sibling might require more attention, and that this does not mean their parents are being unfair. The development of empathy plays a crucial role in this more sophisticated understanding of fairness.

3. Internalizing Moral Values (Ages 10+):

As children enter late childhood and adolescence, they begin to internalize ethical principles, such as justice, responsibility, and honesty. These values often reflect the norms of their family, culture, and society. However, as they grow more independent, they start forming their own moral judgments, especially when faced with ethical dilemmas or conflicting values.

Moral Challenges During Adolescence

Adolescence is a critical period for moral development as teenagers start questioning authority, societal norms, and their personal values. This phase of moral exploration can lead to moral conflicts and challenges.

1. Identity and Moral Values:

During adolescence, individuals engage in the process of identity formation, which includes determining their moral and ethical beliefs. Adolescents may question the values they've been taught and explore alternative viewpoints. This can lead to moral conflicts, particularly if their emerging beliefs clash with those of their family or peers.

2. Peer Influence on Moral Decision-Making:

Peer pressure can significantly influence adolescents' moral choices. Adolescents are highly sensitive to peer approval, and this can sometimes lead to engaging in behaviors that conflict with their internal moral compass, such as lying, cheating, or participating in risky activities. Studies show that adolescents are more likely to take moral risks in group settings due to the influence of peers.

3. Moral Dilemmas and Personal Integrity:

Adolescents begin facing more complex moral dilemmas, such as deciding whether to stand up against bullying, resist peer pressure, or choose between competing values like loyalty and honesty. How they navigate these dilemmas plays a key role in their moral identity formation and ethical development.

Action Plans to Foster Moral Development

Supporting moral development in children and adolescents requires intentional efforts from parents, educators, and society. Below are some actionable steps to promote moral growth:

1. **Encourage Open Discussions About Ethics:**

   Create an environment where children and teenagers feel comfortable discussing moral dilemmas and ethical questions. By engaging in conversations about fairness, honesty, and responsibility, caregivers can help children refine their moral reasoning.

2. **Model Ethical Behavior:**

   Children learn by observing the behavior of adults. Parents, teachers, and caregivers should model ethical behavior, such as fairness, empathy, and integrity. Demonstrating moral decision-making in everyday life helps children internalize these values.

3. **Teach Empathy and Perspective-Taking:**

   Empathy is a key component of moral development. Encourage children to consider other people's perspectives by asking how others might feel in various situations. Activities like role-playing or reading stories about moral conflicts can help children develop empathy.

4. **Provide Opportunities for Moral Practice:**

Allow children to practice moral reasoning in real-life situations. For example, involve them in community service or give them responsibilities that require ethical decision-making. Adolescents, in particular, benefit from engaging in activities that allow them to explore their values and apply them in meaningful ways.

Conclusion

Moral development is a complex, gradual process that begins in early childhood and continues through adolescence. Understanding the theories proposed by Kohlberg and Piaget helps us appreciate how children progress from simple rule-following to more sophisticated moral reasoning. As they grow, children develop a sense of ethics and fairness, influenced by their environment, peers, and personal experiences. Adolescence presents its own unique set of challenges, as teenagers explore their identity and moral values amidst peer influence and societal expectations.

By fostering open discussions, modeling ethical behavior, teaching empathy, and providing real-world opportunities to practice moral decision-making, we can support children and adolescents in developing strong moral foundations. These moral principles will guide them throughout their lives, helping them navigate complex social situations and contributing to their growth as responsible, ethical individuals.

Dr.Y.Narasimha Raja

Chapter 10: Influence of Family and Culture on Child Development

"Children are not born with instructions. They develop in response to the love, care, and guidance they receive from their family and culture." — Anonymous

Influence of Family and Culture on Child development.

Child development is shaped by various factors, with family and culture playing pivotal roles. Families provide the initial environment in which children learn, grow, and form their early perceptions of the world. Parenting styles, the presence of siblings, and the broader cultural context in which a child is raised all influence their cognitive, emotional, and social development. According to the World Health Organization (WHO), family and cultural environments are key determinants in child development, as they shape a child's values, behaviors, and emotional resilience. This chapter delves into how family and culture influence child development by exploring the psychological impacts of parenting styles, the role of siblings, cultural variations in child-rearing practices, and the effects of family dynamics on emotional growth.

Parenting Styles and Their Psychological Impact

"The way we talk to our children becomes their inner voice." — Peggy O'Mara

The way parents interact with their children significantly influences their psychological development. Developmental psychologist Diana Baumrind identified four main parenting styles: authoritative, authoritarian, permissive, and neglectful. Each style has a distinct impact on a child's emotional, social, and cognitive growth.

Authoritative Parenting: Authoritative parents are warm, supportive, and responsive, but they also set clear boundaries and expectations. Research shows that children raised in authoritative households tend to have higher self-esteem, better social skills, and are more independent. This style encourages children to explore their autonomy within a structured environment, which promotes healthy emotional development. A study published in the Journal of Adolescence found that authoritative parenting is linked to better academic outcomes and lower levels of anxiety in children.

Authoritarian Parenting: Authoritarian parents are highly controlling and expect strict obedience from their children, often with little emotional warmth or flexibility. While this style may ensure immediate compliance, it can lead to negative outcomes such as low self-esteem, difficulty in social interactions, and increased likelihood of anxiety or depression. Children raised in authoritarian environments may struggle with decision-making and may become overly dependent on authority figures for validation.

Permissive Parenting: Permissive parents are indulgent and lenient, often avoiding discipline or setting few limits for their children. While this style may create a nurturing and affectionate environment, it can also lead to a lack of self-discipline in children. Studies show that children raised in permissive households may have difficulty managing their emotions and are more likely to engage in problematic behaviors, such as substance abuse, later in life.

Neglectful Parenting: Neglectful parents are disengaged, offering little guidance or emotional support to their children. This style can have severe consequences for child development, leading to attachment issues, poor academic performance, and difficulty forming healthy relationships. Children in neglectful homes often feel unsupported and may exhibit behavioral issues or emotional instability.

The Role of Siblings in Child Development

Siblings often serve as a child's first companions, role models, and rivals. Their influence on development is profound, affecting emotional regulation, social skills, and even academic achievement.

Emotional and Social Learning: Siblings provide opportunities for children to learn about empathy, negotiation, and conflict resolution. Through sibling interactions, children experience both competition and cooperation, which helps them develop important social skills. A study from the Journal of Family Psychology suggests that positive sibling relationships can enhance a child's emotional resilience and social competence, while sibling rivalry can teach conflict management.

Sibling Role Models: Older siblings often serve as role models for younger children, influencing their academic achievements, social behaviors, and even risk-taking tendencies. Younger siblings may imitate their older siblings' behaviors, whether positive or negative. This modeling can either encourage healthy behaviors, such as studying or participating in sports, or introduce negative behaviors, depending on the older sibling's actions.

Birth Order Effects: The impact of birth order on development is a debated topic. Some theories suggest that first-born children tend to be more responsible and achievement-oriented, while younger siblings may be more socially adept and rebellious. Though these generalizations are not universal, birth order can influence how children perceive their role within the family and society.

Cultural Differences in Child-Rearing Practices

Collectivist vs. Individualist Cultures: In collectivist cultures, such as those in many parts of Asia, Africa, and Latin America, child-rearing practices emphasize interdependence, community responsibility, and respect for authority. Children are often raised with a strong sense of duty to the family and community, and obedience to elders is highly valued. In contrast, individualist cultures, such as those in North America and parts of Europe, focus on fostering independence, self-expression, and personal achievement.

Discipline and Communication Styles: Cultural differences also manifest in disciplinary practices. For example, some cultures may endorse stricter, more authoritarian methods of discipline, believing that these practices instill respect and discipline in children. Other cultures may adopt more permissive or authoritative approaches, focusing on open communication and reasoning with children. A global survey by UNICEF in 2020 found that cultural views on corporal punishment vary widely, with some societies viewing it as an acceptable form of discipline, while others actively discourage it.

Value Systems: Cultural values such as collectivism, honor, respect for tradition, or autonomy shape how children are raised. In some cultures, children are taught to prioritize family needs over their own, while in others, self-reliance is encouraged from a young age. These value systems have lasting impacts on children's behavior, their emotional development, and how they interact with the broader world.

Family Dynamics and Their Effect on Emotional Growth

"Family is not an important thing, it's everything." —
Michael J. Fox

Family dynamics, including the relationships between parents, siblings, and extended family members, play a critical role in a child's emotional development. Healthy family dynamics provide a secure base from which children can explore the world, while dysfunctional dynamics can lead to emotional struggles.

The Importance of Attachment: Secure attachment, particularly with primary caregivers, is essential for a child's emotional development. A positive emotional connection with caregivers allows children to feel safe and supported, fostering self-confidence and emotional regulation. Children who experience inconsistent or negative family dynamics, such as frequent conflict or emotional neglect, are more likely to develop issues related to anxiety, depression, or behavioral problems.

Parental Conflict and Its Impact: Children who are exposed to high levels of parental conflict or divorce may experience stress, insecurity, and confusion. Studies indicate that children from high-conflict homes are more likely to struggle with emotional regulation and may have difficulty forming healthy relationships later in life. It is not the divorce or separation itself that affects children negatively, but the ongoing conflict or lack of emotional support that can cause lasting emotional damage.

Extended Family Influence: In many cultures, extended family members such as grandparents, aunts, and uncles play an active role in a child's upbringing. The presence of extended family can provide additional emotional support and serve as role models, contributing positively to the child's emotional growth. However, conflicting views between parents and extended family members on child-rearing practices can also create confusion for the child.

Action Plans to Overcome Family and Cultural Challenges in Child Development

Parenting Education Programs: Offer parenting workshops that educate caregivers on the impact of different parenting styles and family dynamics. These programs can help parents understand how their behaviors and interactions affect their child's development and provide tools for positive communication and discipline.

Fostering Healthy Sibling Relationships: Encourage activities that promote positive sibling interactions, such as cooperative games and shared responsibilities. Parents should mediate sibling conflicts constructively and teach children conflict resolution skills to build stronger, supportive sibling bonds.

Cultural Sensitivity in Education: Educational institutions should recognize and respect cultural diversity in child-rearing practices. Schools can integrate cultural competence training for teachers, helping them understand and support the varied cultural backgrounds of their students.

Strengthening Family Dynamics: Provide family counseling services to address dysfunctional family dynamics, including parental conflict or communication breakdowns. Encouraging open communication within families can lead to healthier emotional environments for children.

Conclusion

Family and culture are powerful influences on child development, shaping everything from emotional resilience to social competence. Parenting styles, sibling relationships, cultural traditions, and family dynamics all interact to create the foundation for a child's cognitive, emotional, and social growth. By understanding these influences, parents, educators, and caregivers can foster healthier environments that support a child's well-being and development.

Ultimately, by promoting positive family interactions, cultural awareness, and supportive parenting practices, we can guide children towards becoming well-adjusted, compassionate, and resilient adults.

Chapter 11
The Role of Education in Child Psychology

"Education is not the filling of a pail, but the lighting of a fire." — William Butler Yeats

Role of education in child development

Education plays a pivotal role in shaping a child's psychological, social, and cognitive development. From the earliest experiences in a learning environment to the influence of formal schooling, education serves as a critical framework for developing not only academic skills but also emotional intelligence, social behaviors, and self-concept. According to UNICEF, children's formative years—particularly early childhood education—are critical, as 90% of brain development occurs before the age of five. Schooling influences more than academic achievement; it molds a child's self-esteem, resilience, and social integration.

Dr.Y.Narasimha Raja

The Psychological Impact of Schooling

Schooling has a profound influence on children's psychological development, providing both opportunities for growth and potential challenges. A school environment is where children learn not only academic knowledge but also social skills, emotional regulation, and self-concept.

Socialization and Emotional Growth: Schools are primary socialization agents for children. Within this environment, children learn to cooperate, resolve conflicts, and form friendships. Research shows that children who succeed socially in school tend to have higher self-esteem and fewer emotional problems. Schools also help children develop resilience by teaching them to cope with setbacks, whether academic or social.

Academic Pressure and Stress: While schools offer opportunities for growth, they can also be sources of stress. Academic pressure, performance expectations, and competition can cause anxiety and negatively affect a child's psychological well-being. A 2020 survey by the American Psychological Association (APA) found that school-related stress is one of the top stressors for children and adolescents, often leading to anxiety or burnout.

Self-Esteem and School Success: A child's academic achievements are closely tied to their self-concept and self-esteem. Children who struggle academically may begin to see themselves as less capable, which can lead to feelings of frustration and a decrease in motivation. In contrast, children who excel academically tend to feel more confident and are more likely to engage in learning activities.

Early Childhood Education: Learning through Play

"Play is the highest form of research." — Albert Einstein

Early childhood education (ECE) is foundational for later development, and much of this learning happens through play. Play-based learning allows children to explore the world around them, develop problem-solving skills, and express their emotions.

Cognitive and Emotional Development: Play is a crucial vehicle for cognitive and emotional growth in young children. According to the National Association for the Education of Young Children (NAEYC), play helps children develop language skills, memory, and concentration. Through imaginative play, children also process complex emotions and situations, which aids in emotional regulation and social understanding.

Social Skills Development: Play-based learning also fosters social interaction. Group play encourages cooperation, sharing, and the development of empathy. For instance, when children play together in structured or unstructured activities, they learn how to navigate social rules, negotiate roles, and resolve conflicts, all of which are essential for healthy psychological development.

Creativity and Problem-Solving: Creative play allows children to engage in problem-solving and critical thinking. Building blocks, puzzles, and pretend scenarios help children think creatively and improve their cognitive flexibility. These skills are important for later academic success and emotional resilience.

Dr.Y.Narasimha Raja

The Role of Teachers in Psychological Development

Teachers are among the most influential figures in a child's life, second only to parents. Their influence extends beyond academic instruction and reaches into the psychological realm, impacting a child's emotional, social, and intellectual growth.

Teacher-Student Relationships:A positive, supportive relationship between teachers and students can foster emotional security and boost academic motivation. Teachers who create an emotionally safe and encouraging classroom environment help children feel valued and understood, which promotes self-confidence. Studies published by the American Educational Research Journal indicate that children who feel supported by their teachers are more likely to be engaged in school and experience better mental health outcomes.

Teachers as Role Models: Teachers serve as role models for behavior, social interaction, and emotional regulation. Children often look to their teachers for guidance on how to handle challenges, respond to setbacks, and manage emotions. Teachers who demonstrate patience, kindness, and fairness encourage similar behaviors in their students, contributing to a positive school climate and fostering emotional intelligence.

Fostering Resilience and Independence: Teachers play a critical role in helping children develop resilience and independence. By providing structured opportunities for problem-solving, encouraging self-directed learning, and supporting perseverance, teachers help students build the psychological tools necessary for overcoming obstacles both inside and outside the classroom.

Learning Disabilities and Special Educational Needs

Children with learning disabilities or special educational needs (SEN) face unique challenges in the classroom that can affect their psychological well-being. These challenges require tailored interventions to ensure that all children, regardless of their learning abilities, receive the support they need to succeed.

Understanding Learning Disabilities: Learning disabilities, such as dyslexia, ADHD, and dyscalculia, affect how children process information. These difficulties can lead to frustration, lower self-esteem, and academic underachievement if not identified and addressed early. According to the Learning Disabilities Association of America, 5-15% of school-aged children struggle with some form of learning disability.

Psychological Impact of Learning Disabilities: Children with learning disabilities often feel isolated or stigmatized in a traditional classroom setting, which can lead to anxiety, depression, and behavioral issues. They may internalize their struggles as personal failures, rather than understanding them as specific challenges that can be addressed with the right support.

Special Educational Needs and Inclusion: Children with special educational needs require individualized learning plans that cater to their unique abilities. Inclusive education, where children with SEN are integrated into mainstream classrooms with appropriate support, has been shown to improve both academic outcomes and psychological well-being. Teachers who adapt their teaching methods to meet the diverse needs of all students contribute to a more inclusive and supportive learning environment.

Action Plans to Overcome Challenges in Education and Child Psychology

Promote Mental Health Support in Schools: Schools should implement mental health programs and provide access to counselors or psychologists who can help children manage academic pressure, stress, and emotional challenges. Early intervention can prevent long-term psychological issues.

Enhance Teacher Training: Teachers should receive training in child psychology, emotional intelligence, and learning disabilities to better understand and respond to the diverse psychological needs of their students. This will enable teachers to create emotionally supportive and inclusive classrooms.

Implement Play-Based Learning in Early Childhood Education: Encourage early childhood education programs to incrporate more play-based learning activities that promote cognitive, social, and emotional development. Play should be recognized as a valuable educational tool, particularly for young children.

Conclusion Education is one of the most significant factors influencing a child's psychological development. Schools serve as environments where children learn not only academic skills but also social, emotional, and behavioral competencies that shape their overall well-being. The psychological impact of schooling, the benefits of early childhood education through play, and the critical role of teachers in fostering emotional resilience are essential components of a child's development.

Chapter 12
Child Mental Health and Well-being

"Mental health is not a destination, but a process. It's about how you drive, not where you're going."
— Noam Shpancer

Child mental health is a crucial but often overlooked aspect of child development. As children grow and develop, they encounter various emotional, social, and psychological challenges that can impact their mental well-being. According to the World Health Organization (WHO), around 10-20% of children and adolescents worldwide experience mental health disorders, with anxiety and depression being among the most common. Recognizing and addressing mental health issues early in childhood is essential to prevent long-term emotional and psychological challenges. This chapter explores key areas of child mental health, including recognizing and supporting childhood anxiety and depression, understanding childhood trauma and its interventions, the role of play therapy, and building resilience in children.

Dr.Y.Narasimha Raja

Recognizing and Supporting Childhood Anxiety and Depression

Childhood anxiety and depression are significant mental health challenges that can impact a child's overall development. While these conditions were once believed to primarily affect adults, recent studies show that anxiety and depression are becoming increasingly common among children.

1. Recognizing Anxiety and Depression in Children:

Symptoms of childhood anxiety often include excessive worry, irritability, difficulty sleeping, and avoidance of certain situations or activities. Depression in children may manifest as persistent sadness, withdrawal from social interactions, loss of interest in previously enjoyed activities, and changes in appetite or sleep patterns. According to a study published by the National Institute of Mental Health (NIMH), about 7.1% of children aged 3 to 17 experience anxiety, while 3.2% are affected by depression.

2. Supporting Children with Anxiety and Depression:

Early intervention is crucial for managing childhood anxiety and depression. Supportive strategies include creating a safe and nurturing environment where children feel comfortable expressing their emotions. Cognitive-behavioral therapy (CBT) is often used to help children challenge negative thought patterns and develop coping strategies. Parental involvement is also essential in providing emotional support and fostering open communication about feelings.

"You cannot stop the waves, but you can learn to surf." — Jon Kabat-Zinn

Childhood Trauma: Causes, Symptoms, and Interventions

Childhood trauma can have profound effects on a child's emotional and psychological development. Trauma can arise from a variety of experiences, such as abuse, neglect, domestic violence, the loss of a loved one, or exposure to disasters or accidents.

1. Causes and Symptoms of Childhood Trauma: Traumatic experiences can leave lasting scars on a child's mental health. Children who have experienced trauma may exhibit symptoms such as nightmares, flashbacks, emotional numbness, difficulty concentrating, or aggressive behavior. A report by the National Child Traumatic Stress Network (NCTSN) indicates that over two-thirds of children in the U.S. report experiencing at least one traumatic event by age 16. Trauma can disrupt a child's sense of safety and lead to feelings of helplessness, anxiety, and depression.

2. Interventions for Childhood Trauma: Effective interventions for childhood trauma often involve trauma-focused cognitive-behavioral therapy (TF-CBT), which helps children process their traumatic experiences in a safe and supportive environment. Family therapy can also be beneficial, as it fosters communication and healing within the family unit. Creating stability and routine for the child is key to helping them regain a sense of safety and control over their environment.

"Trauma is a fact of life. It does not, however, have to be a life sentence." — Peter A. Levine

The Role of Play Therapy in Treating Emotional Difficulties

Play therapy is a widely used therapeutic approach that allows children to express their emotions and resolve psychological difficulties through play. Play is a natural medium for children to communicate and process their thoughts and feelings, particularly when they are unable to verbalize complex emotions.

1. How Play Therapy Works:

Play therapy provides a safe, non-threatening environment where children can express their emotions and experiences through toys, games, and creative activities. Through guided play, therapists observe the child's behavior and help them work through emotional difficulties. Play therapy is particularly effective for children who have experienced trauma, anxiety, depression, or behavioral problems.

2. Benefits of Play Therapy:

Play therapy promotes emotional expression, improves problem-solving skills, and enhances a child's ability to cope with stress. It also encourages children to explore their emotions in a way that feels comfortable and familiar. According to the Association for Play Therapy (APT), children who participate in play therapy often show improvements in their emotional and behavioral functioning, as well as enhanced self-esteem and social skills.

"Play gives children a chance to practice what they are learning." —
Fred Rogers

Building Resilience in Children

Resilience is the ability to bounce back from adversity and cope with life's challenges. Building resilience in children is a key component of promoting long-term mental well-being, as it equips them with the skills to navigate difficult situations.

1. Factors that Promote Resilience:

Resilience is shaped by both internal and external factors. Internally, a child's temperament, self-regulation skills, and problem-solving abilities play a role in their resilience. Externally, supportive relationships with caregivers, teachers, and peers are crucial for fostering resilience. A study published in the Journal of Child Psychology and Psychiatry found that children who have at least one strong, supportive relationship with an adult are more likely to develop resilience.

2. Strategies for Building Resilience:

To help children build resilience, caregivers and educators can encourage a growth mindset, where children learn to view challenges as opportunities for growth. Providing children with opportunities to make decisions, solve problems, and take risks in a safe environment also promotes resilience. Teaching emotional regulation techniques, such as mindfulness or deep breathing exercises, helps children manage stress and build coping mechanisms for difficult emotions.

"Do not judge me by my success, judge me by how many times I fell down and got back up again." — Nelson Mandela

Action Plans to Overcome Mental Health Challenges in Children

1. **Raise Awareness and Reduce Stigma:**

Mental health education should be a priority in schools and communities to raise awareness about childhood mental health issues. By reducing the stigma associated with mental health, children and their families may feel more comfortable seeking help when needed.

2. **Implement School-Based Mental Health Programs:**

Schools should provide access to mental health resources, including school counselors, psychologists, and support groups. School-based programs that teach emotional regulation, stress management, and social skills can foster a supportive environment for children to manage their mental health.

3. **Early Intervention and Support Services:**

Early identification of mental health issues, such as anxiety, depression, or trauma, is critical. Pediatricians, teachers, and parents should work together to recognize signs of emotional distress and seek early intervention. Referrals to mental health professionals and access to appropriate therapies, such as cognitive-behavioral therapy or play therapy, can help address these challenges.

4. **Strengthen Parental Involvement:**

Parents play a vital role in supporting their child's mental health. Educating parents on how to communicate with their children about emotions, manage stress, and create a nurturing home environment is essential for promoting mental well-being. Parenting workshops or family counseling services can be valuable resources for parents.

Conclusion

Child mental health and well-being are foundational to a child's overall development and quality of life. Recognizing and addressing mental health issues such as anxiety, depression, and trauma in childhood is critical for promoting emotional resilience and healthy psychological growth. Through therapeutic interventions like play therapy and the cultivation of resilience, children can learn to navigate life's challenges with confidence and emotional strength.

By fostering a supportive environment both at home and in schools, and by providing access to early intervention and mental health resources, we can ensure that children have the tools they need to develop a strong sense of mental well-being. Addressing child mental health proactively is not just about treating problems as they arise, but about equipping children with the emotional and psychological resilience to thrive throughout their lives.

Chapter-13
The Digital Age: Technology & Child Psychology

"Technology will never replace great teachers, but in the hands of great teachers, it's transformational." — *George* Couros

In the 21st century, technology has woven itself into the fabric of everyday life, profoundly shaping the experiences of children. While technology provides countless opportunities for learning, entertainment, and connection, its growing influence also raises concerns about its impact on child development, mental health, and social behavior. According to the American Academy of Pediatrics, children and teenagers are now exposed to screens for an average of seven hours per day, with screen time increasing year after year. Understanding the impact of screen time, social media, and the potential risks of digital addiction is crucial for promoting healthy development. This chapter explores the relationship between technology and child psychology, focusing on screen time's effects, social media's influence on adolescents, technology as a learning tool, and strategies for managing digital addiction in children.

The Impact of Screen Time on Development

"It's not just about giving children access to technology but about making sure they are using it in ways that promote learning, health, and positive social behavior." — *Sonia Livingstone*

Screen time, whether it's through smartphones, tablets, computers, or television, has become a dominant activity in children's daily lives. However, the effects of prolonged screen time on child development can be both positive and negative, depending on the type of content consumed and the time spent on digital devices.

Cognitive and Language Development: Excessive screen time, particularly in early childhood, has been linked to delays in language and cognitive development. Studies suggest that children under two who are exposed to excessive screen time may experience difficulties with language acquisition and attention. According to a study published in JAMA Pediatrics, children who spend more than two hours a day on screens score lower on language and cognitive tests compared to children with limited screen exposure. This is largely because passive screen use, like watching videos, doesn't stimulate interactive language or problem-solving skills as well as real-world interactions.

Physical Development and Health Risks: Increased screen time is associated with physical health risks, such as poor posture, eye strain, and sleep disturbances. Screen time before bed, in particular, can disrupt sleep cycles due to the blue light emitted by devices, which interferes with melatonin production. Furthermore, prolonged sedentary behavior linked to screen time has been correlated with an increased risk of childhood obesity, according to the World Health Organization (WHO).

Social and Emotional Development: Screen time can affect a child's social and emotional development by limiting face-to-face interactions and the development of critical social skills. Children who spend significant time on devices may miss opportunities to engage in peer play, conflict resolution, and emotional learning, all of which are vital for emotional intelligence. Studies also show that children who overuse screens are more likely to exhibit behavioral issues such as hyperactivity, aggression, and difficulty focusing.

Social Media and Its Influence on Adolescents

"Social media allows us to stay connected, but don't let it disconnect you from yourself.

Social media platforms such as Instagram, TikTok, Snapchat, and Facebook have become central to the lives of adolescents, offering them opportunities to connect with friends, share experiences, and explore new interests. However, the influence of social media on adolescent mental health and behavior has sparked growing concern among parents, educators, and mental health professionals.

1.   Impact on Self-Esteem and Body Image:

Social media often presents unrealistic standards of beauty and success, contributing to issues like low self-esteem and body dissatisfaction, particularly among adolescent girls. A study published in The Journal of Adolescence found that adolescents who spend significant time on social media are more likely to compare themselves to others, leading to increased levels of anxiety, depression, and dissatisfaction with their appearance. The constant exposure to "perfect" images and lifestyles can create unrealistic expectations and foster feelings of inadequacy.

2. Cyberbullying and Online Harassment:

The anonymity and distance provided by social media platforms can increase the risk of cyberbullying. Adolescents are particularly vulnerable to online harassment, which can have devastating effects on their self-esteem, mental health, and sense of safety. According to a report by the Pew Research Center, 59% of U.S. teens have experienced some form of cyberbullying, with lasting psychological consequences, including increased anxiety, depression, and in extreme cases, suicidal thoughts.

3. Social Connection or Isolation:

While social media can provide a sense of connection and community, it can also lead to feelings of isolation and loneliness. Adolescents may experience "fear of missing out" (FOMO) as they see friends engaging in activities without them. This can lead to compulsive checking of social media accounts, further deepening feelings of inadequacy and isolation. However, when used appropriately, social media can foster supportive communities where adolescents can connect with like-minded peers and engage in positive interactions.

Dr.Y.Narasimha Raja

Technology as a Tool for Learning

While concerns about the negative effects of technology are valid, it is also important to recognize its potential as a transformative tool for learning.

Interactive and Personalized Learning: Educational apps, software, and online platforms offer personalized learning experiences tailored to a child's specific needs. Adaptive learning technologies can adjust the level of difficulty based on a child's performance, helping them grasp concepts at their own pace. This is particularly beneficial for children with learning disabilities or those who need more time to master skills.

Accessibility to Information and Resources: The internet provides children and adolescents with access to a vast amount of information, from educational videos to virtual museums. This unlimited access allows students to deepen their knowledge on subjects they are passionate about, beyond the classroom. For instance, students can participate in virtual science experiments, explore historical events through interactive timelines, or practice coding using online tutorials.

Encouraging Collaboration and Critical Thinking: Technology also encourages collaboration, with platforms like Google Classroom, Zoom, and Microsoft Teams enabling students to work together on projects in real-time, regardless of physical location. Online discussion forums can promote critical thinking as students debate ideas, share insights, and offer feedback to peers.

"The goal of education is not just to increase the amount of knowledge but to create the possibilities for a child to invent and discover." Jean

Managing Digital Addiction in Children

Digital addiction, characterized by compulsive and excessive use of digital devices, is a growing concern for children and adolescents. When screen time becomes excessive, it can disrupt a child's social, emotional, and academic development, leading to significant challenges.

1. Recognizing Digital Addiction:

Signs of digital addiction in children include difficulty limiting screen time, irritability or anxiety when separated from devices, neglecting responsibilities or hobbies, and withdrawal from social or family interactions. A study by Common Sense Media found that 50% of teens feel addicted to their smartphones, with many reporting anxiety when separated from their devices.

2. Psychological and Behavioral Impact:

Excessive screen use can contribute to a range of mental health issues, including increased anxiety, depression, and attention problems. Additionally, digital addiction can interfere with sleep patterns, reduce physical activity, and limit opportunities for face-to-face social interactions. This can lead to feelings of isolation and difficulty forming real-world relationships.

3. Strategies for Managing Digital Addiction:

Parents and educators can help children manage digital addiction by setting clear boundaries and encouraging balanced tech use. This includes creating "tech-free" zones during meals, setting screen time limits, and promoting offline activities like sports, reading, and family games. It is also important to model healthy digital behavior by demonstrating balanced screen use in the home.

"The greatest wealth is health." — Virgil

Action Plans to Overcome Challenges in the Digital Age

1. **Educate on Digital Literacy:** It's essential to educate children and adolescents on digital literacy, teaching them how to use technology responsibly and how to critically evaluate the information they encounter online. Schools and parents can collaborate to help children understand the potential risks of social media and excessive screen time, as well as the benefits of using technology for learning and personal growth.

2. **Encourage Tech-Free Time:** Parents should establish regular "tech-free" times for children to disconnect from their devices and engage in face-to-face interactions, physical activity, and creative play. This helps children develop social skills and fosters emotional regulation.

3. **Monitor and Guide Social Media Use:**Parents can play an active role in guiding their child's social media use by setting appropriate boundaries and discussing the risks of cyberbullying, online predators, and social comparison. Encouraging open communication about their online experiences can help children navigate social media safely.

4. **Incorporate Technology as a Learning Tool:** Educators should embrace the potential of technology to enhance learning by incorporating interactive tools, apps, and platforms that engage students in critical thinking and problem-solving. Blending traditional teaching methods with technological resources can create a balanced and enriching educational experience.

5. **Address Digital Addiction Early:** Parents and educators should be aware of the signs of digital addiction and intervene early by setting limits and offering support. Encouraging alternative activities, such as outdoor play, reading, or hobbies, can help children develop a more balanced relationship with technology.

Conclusion

The digital age presents both opportunities and challenges for child psychology. While technology offers significant benefits as a tool for learning and social connection, excessive screen time and digital addiction can negatively impact a child's cognitive, emotional, and physical development. Social media, in particular, poses unique risks for adolescents, influencing their self-esteem, mental health, and social behavior.

By fostering digital literacy, setting boundaries for screen use, and embracing technology's educational potential, parents, educators, and caregivers can help children navigate the complexities of the digital world. The goal is not to eliminate technology from children's lives but to guide them in using it responsibly and healthily, ensuring it contributes positively to their overall development and well-being.

Chapter 14
Gender Identity and Child Development

"It is time for parents to teach young people early on that in diversity, there is beauty and there is strength." — Maya Angelou

Gender identity is a fundamental aspect of human development and begins to form in early childhood. It refers to an individual's personal sense of their gender, which may or may not align with the sex they were assigned at birth. In recent years, conversations around gender have evolved, with growing recognition of the diversity in gender identities and expressions.

Understanding Gender Roles in Childhood

From a very young age, children are exposed to gender roles—societal expectations and norms about how boys and girls should behave, dress, and interact. These roles are often reinforced by parents, teachers, media, and culture, shaping children's understanding of what it means to be "male" or "female."

Early Gender Role Socialization: Children begin learning about gender roles through their surroundings and observations. Gender-specific toys, clothing, and activities are often presented to children from infancy. Boys may be encouraged to play with trucks and engage in rough-and-tumble play, while girls may be steered toward dolls and nurturing activities. A study published in Developmental Psychology suggests that by age two, children start to show preferences for gender-typed toys, and by age three, they have a basic understanding of gender categories.

The Impact of Gender Stereotypes: Rigid gender roles can limit children's exploration of their interests and talents. For instance, boys may feel discouraged from expressing emotions, while girls may avoid activities perceived as "masculine," like sports or science. These stereotypes can restrict personal growth and create unnecessary barriers to emotional and cognitive development. Encouraging flexibility in gender roles allows children to explore a broader range of activities, fostering a more balanced development of their skills and interests.

The Development of Gender Identity & Expression

Gender Identity Formation: Children typically begin to develop a stable sense of their gender identity between ages 3 and 6. This process involves recognizing oneself as male, female, or something else, and understanding that gender is a permanent aspect of their identity. While most children's gender identity aligns with their biological sex, some may experience a disconnect, identifying as a different gender or as non-binary. According to research by the Williams Institute, approximately 0.7% of adolescents in the United States identify as transgender.

Exploration and Expression of Gender: During early childhood, children may experiment with gender expression by exploring different styles of dress or playing with toys traditionally associated with another gender. This exploration is a natural part of development and should be supported rather than discouraged. For example, a boy dressing up as a princess or a girl playing with toy cars should be viewed as a healthy exploration of identity rather than something to be corrected.

The Role of Culture and Family: Cultural and family attitudes toward gender can significantly influence how children express their gender. In more rigidly gendered cultures, children may face pressure to conform to traditional gender roles.

Addressing Gender-Related Issues in Adolescence

Adolescence is a critical period for identity formation, including gender identity. During this time, young people often experience heightened awareness of their gender and may confront societal expectations or personal challenges related to their gender identity.

Gender Dysphoria in Adolescence: Some adolescents may experience gender dysphoria, a psychological condition in which there is a significant disconnect between their gender identity and the sex they were assigned at birth. This can lead to feelings of discomfort, anxiety, and depression.

Peer Pressure and Bullying: Adolescents who express gender non-conforming behaviors may face bullying, exclusion, or discrimination from peers. Research published in The Journal of Adolescent Health found that transgender and gender-nonconforming adolescents are at a higher risk for bullying, which can lead to mental health issues like anxiety, depression, and suicidal ideation.

Role of Support Networks: Support from family, friends, and educators plays a critical role in helping adolescents navigate gender-related challenges. Parents and teachers who affirm a young person's gender identity can significantly reduce the risk of mental health problems.

Action Plans to Overcome Gender-Related Challenges

Promote Gender-Inclusive Education: Schools should implement gender-inclusive curricula that educate students about gender diversity and promote respect for all identities. Teachers can create gender-neutral spaces and avoid reinforcing traditional gender roles, ensuring that all students feel valued and included.

Support Family Education and Awareness: Providing resources and support for families is crucial for the well-being of children exploring their gender identity. Parenting workshops and counseling services can help families understand and support their child's gender exploration in a positive and affirming way.

Encourage Open Dialogue and Safe Spaces: Both at home and in schools, fostering open conversations about gender identity and providing safe spaces for children and adolescents to express themselves is essential. Support groups and peer networks can provide LGBTQ+ youth with the validation and community they need to thrive.

Conclusion

Gender identity plays a crucial role in the development of children and adolescents, influencing their sense of self and how they navigate the world. Understanding the complexities of gender roles, supporting healthy exploration of gender identity and expression, and addressing gender-related challenges in adolescence are essential steps in promoting the well-being of all children.

Chapter 15
Adolescence & Emotional Turmoil

"Adolescence is a new birth, for the higher and more completely human traits are now born." — G. Stanley

Adolescence is often characterized as a period of intense emotional and psychological change, marked by the challenges of transitioning from childhood to adulthood. This stage is one of the most turbulent in human development, driven by biological, social, and cognitive changes. According to the World Health Organization (WHO), approximately 1.2 billion people worldwide are adolescents, and they face unique mental health challenges, with an estimated 10-20% experiencing mental health conditions during this time. Adolescence is also a critical period for the formation of identity, autonomy, and independence, but it is often accompanied by emotional turmoil, peer pressure, and risk-taking behavior. This chapter explores the psychological impact of puberty, the causes and solutions for adolescent rebellion, the influence of peer pressure and risk-taking behavior, and the search for identity and independence.

The Psychological Impact of Puberty

Puberty is the biological process that marks the beginning of adolescence, characterized by physical changes such as growth spurts, the development of secondary sexual characteristics, and hormonal shifts.

Hormonal Changes and Emotional Sensitivity:
As adolescents enter puberty, they experience a surge in hormones, including testosterone and estrogen, which affect mood regulation. These hormonal changes can make adolescents more emotionally reactive, leading to increased irritability, anxiety, and mood swings. The American Psychological Association notes that these hormonal fluctuations contribute to the emotional sensitivity commonly observed in adolescents, particularly during the early stages of puberty.

Body Image and Self-Esteem: Physical changes during puberty, such as changes in body shape, skin conditions, and weight gain, can lead to concerns about body image. Adolescents often compare themselves to peers and media portrayals of beauty, which can negatively affect self-esteem. A 2020 study in the Journal of Adolescence found that adolescents who are dissatisfied with their body image are at greater risk for developing eating disorders, depression, and low self-worth.

Cognitive Development and Abstract Thinking: Adolescence also marks a shift in cognitive development, with the emergence of abstract thinking. This allows adolescents to reflect more deeply on themselves and the world around them, leading to heightened self-consciousness and introspection. While this cognitive shift enables growth in reasoning and problem-solving, it can also lead to overthinking, increased self-doubt, and feelings of insecurity.

Dr.Y.Narasimha Raja

Adolescent Rebellion: Causes and Solutions

Adolescent rebellion is often seen as a natural part of growing up, where teenagers push against boundaries and assert their independence.

Causes of Adolescent Rebellion: The need for autonomy is one of the primary drivers of adolescent rebellion. As teenagers strive to develop their own identities, they often feel constrained by rules and expectations set by adults. Additionally, cognitive development during adolescence enables them to question authority, challenge norms, and form their own opinions, often leading to disagreements with parents or teachers. Emotional instability, peer influence, and a desire for independence further contribute to rebellious behavior.

Manifestations of Rebellion: Rebellion in adolescents can take many forms, including defiance of rules, experimenting with risky behaviors (such as substance use), or engaging in conflict with authority figures. For some teens, rebellion may manifest as withdrawal or isolation from family, while others may express it through more overt actions such as breaking curfew or disregarding school responsibilities.

Solutions to Address Rebellion: Understanding that adolescent rebellion is rooted in a desire for autonomy is key to addressing it. Parents and teachers can respond by providing adolescents with appropriate opportunities for independence while maintaining boundaries. Collaborative problem-solving, open communication, and mutual respect can help ease tensions. Allowing adolescents to voice their concerns and participate in decision-making fosters a sense of responsibility and control over their lives.

Peer Pressure and Risk-Taking Behavior

Peer pressure is a powerful force during adolescence, as teenagers place great importance on acceptance and belonging within their social circles. This desire for social inclusion often influences behavior, including the tendency to engage in risk-taking activities.

The Influence of Peer Pressure: Adolescents are highly influenced by their peers, who shape their attitudes, values, and behaviors. While peer relationships can provide emotional support and companionship, they can also encourage risky behaviors. Adolescents may feel pressured to engage in activities such as smoking, drinking, drug use, or reckless driving to fit in with their peers. The National Institute on Drug Abuse reports that peer pressure is one of the leading factors contributing to substance use among adolescents.

Risk-Taking Behavior and Its Causes

Risk-taking behavior is common during adolescence due to the underdevelopment of the prefrontal cortex, the brain region responsible for impulse control and decision-making.

Strategies to Address Peer Pressure and Risk-Taking: Educating adolescents about the potential consequences of risky behavior is an important step in reducing peer pressure's influence. Parents and educators should foster environments where adolescents feel supported and empowered to make informed decisions. Providing adolescents with healthy outlets for risk-taking, such as sports or creative activities, can also help reduce the likelihood of engaging in dangerous behaviors.

The Search for Identity & Independence

Adolescence is a critical period for identity formation, as teenagers begin to explore who they are and how they fit into the world. This search for identity is intertwined with the desire for independence from parents and societal expectations.

Erikson's Theory of Identity vs. Role Confusion: Psychologist Erik Erikson identified adolescence as the stage of "identity vs. role confusion," where individuals work to form a coherent sense of self. During this time, adolescents may experiment with different roles, values, and identities in search of a true sense of self. This process can be complicated by external pressures from parents, schools, and peer groups, leading to periods of confusion or uncertainty.

The Role of Exploration in Identity Formation: Exploration is a vital component of identity development. Adolescents may experiment with different interests, friendships, styles, and belief systems as part of their journey to discover who they are. While this exploration is a natural and healthy process, it can also be a source of anxiety as adolescents grapple with uncertainty and self-doubt.

Supporting the Search for Identity: Parents and educators can support adolescents in their search for identity by providing guidance without imposing rigid expectations. Encouraging self-reflection, open dialogue, and exploration of various interests and ideas can help adolescents develop a strong sense of self. It's important to allow adolescents the space to make mistakes and learn from their experiences, as this contributes to the formation of a mature and independent identity.

Action Plans to Overcome Challenges of Adolescence

Fostering Open Communication: Parents and educators should maintain open lines of communication with adolescents, encouraging them to express their thoughts and feelings. Listening without judgment helps adolescents feel supported and less inclined to rebel or withdraw.

Providing Healthy Outlets for Risk-Taking: To address the adolescent need for novelty and risk, provide opportunities for positive risk-taking, such as participating in sports, the arts, or community service. These activities allow adolescents to test their limits in a controlled and supportive environment.

Conclusion

Adolescence is a period of significant emotional, social, and cognitive development, often marked by emotional turmoil, rebellion, peer pressure, and the search for identity. Understanding the psychological impact of puberty, the causes of adolescent rebellion, and the influence of peer pressure can help parents, educators, and caregivers support adolescents through this challenging time. By fostering open communication, promoting healthy risk-taking, and encouraging self-exploration, we can guide adolescents toward developing a strong sense of self and emotional resilience.

Adolescence is not just a phase of difficulty, but a time of opportunity for growth, learning, and the emergence of a more mature and independent individual. With the right support, adolescents can navigate this turbulent period and emerge stronger, more confident, and better prepared for adulthood.

Chapter 16
Childhood Disorders and Their Management

"Children are not things to be molded, but are people to be unfolded." — Jess Lair

Childhood is a critical stage for emotional, cognitive, and social development. However, for some children, this period can be marked by the onset of developmental, behavioral, and emotional disorders. According to the World Health Organization (WHO), approximately 10-20% of children and adolescents globally experience mental health disorders. These disorders, if left untreated, can lead to long-term difficulties in academic performance, social interaction, and overall well-being. Autism Spectrum Disorder (ASD), Attention Deficit Hyperactivity Disorder (ADHD), anxiety, depression, and Obsessive-Compulsive Disorder (OCD) are among the most common childhood mental health disorders. This chapter focuses on understanding these disorders, their management, and strategies to support affected children and their families.

Autism Spectrum Disorder: Understanding and Supporting

Autism Spectrum Disorder (ASD) is a developmental disorder that affects communication, social interaction, and behavior. The spectrum nature of the condition means that symptoms can range from mild to severe, with each individual presenting a unique set of challenges.

Understanding Autism Spectrum Disorder:ASD typically becomes apparent in early childhood, with signs such as delayed speech, difficulty maintaining eye contact, repetitive behaviors, and trouble understanding social cues. According to the Centers for Disease Control and Prevention (CDC), about 1 in 54 children in the U.S. is diagnosed with ASD. The exact causes of autism are still not fully understood, but research suggests that a combination of genetic and environmental factors contributes to the condition.

Supporting Children with ASD: Support for children with ASD includes individualized approaches tailored to their specific needs. Early intervention is crucial in helping children develop communication, social, and behavioral skills. Therapies such as Applied Behavior Analysis (ABA), speech therapy, and occupational therapy are commonly used to support development. In addition to professional interventions, parents and caregivers can provide support by creating structured routines, using visual aids for communication, and fostering a supportive environment that encourages social interaction.

Dr.Y.Narasimha Raja

ADHD: Diagnosis, Treatment, and Coping Strategies

Attention Deficit Hyperactivity Disorder (ADHD) is a neurodevelopmental disorder characterized by symptoms of inattention, hyperactivity, and impulsivity.

Diagnosing ADHD: ADHD is typically diagnosed during early school years when children display difficulties with attention and behavior in structured environments like classrooms. The disorder affects around 5-7% of children globally, according to the American Psychiatric Association. Diagnosis involves a comprehensive evaluation that includes behavioral observations, interviews with parents and teachers, and standardized rating scales to assess symptoms.

Treatment Options for ADHD: Treatment for ADHD usually involves a combination of behavioral therapy, medication, and lifestyle changes. Medications such as stimulants (e.g., methylphenidate) can help improve attention and reduce hyperactive behavior. Behavioral therapy focuses on teaching children skills to manage their impulses, stay organized, and improve focus. Parent training programs can also help families implement strategies for supporting children with ADHD at home.

Coping Strategies for Children with ADHD: Children with ADHD can benefit from structured routines, clear expectations, and positive reinforcement for appropriate behavior. Breaking tasks into smaller, manageable steps and providing frequent breaks can help improve focus. Teachers and caregivers can use visual schedules, timers, and rewards to help children stay on task and manage their behavior more effectively.

Anxiety &Depression in Children

While anxiety and depression are often associated with adulthood, these mental health disorders can also affect children.

Recognizing Anxiety and Depression in Children: Children with anxiety may exhibit excessive worry, fear, or nervousness that interferes with their daily activities. They may avoid certain situations, have trouble sleeping, or experience physical symptoms like stomachaches or headaches. Depression in children can manifest as persistent sadness, irritability, withdrawal from social activities, changes in appetite or sleep, and a loss of interest in things they once enjoyed. According to the National Institute of Mental Health (NIMH), about 7.1% of children aged 3-17 experience anxiety, and 3.2% experience depression.

Treatment and Support for Childhood Anxiety and Depression: Cognitive-behavioral therapy (CBT) is one of the most effective treatments for anxiety and depression in children, helping them identify negative thought patterns and develop coping skills. In some cases, medication such as selective serotonin reuptake inhibitors (SSRIs) may be prescribed to manage symptoms. Parents and caregivers can support children by creating a safe, nurturing environment where they feel comfortable expressing their feelings. Encouraging physical activity, maintaining a regular routine, and teaching relaxation techniques such as deep breathing can also help alleviate symptoms.

Dr.Y.Narasimha Raja

Childhood OCD and Other Anxiety Disorders

Obsessive-Compulsive Disorder (OCD) is an anxiety disorder characterized by intrusive, unwanted thoughts (obsessions) and repetitive behaviors (compulsions) performed to reduce anxiety. OCD, along with other anxiety disorders like generalized anxiety disorder (GAD) and separation anxiety disorder, can significantly impact a child's quality of life.

Understanding OCD in Children: Children with OCD may experience distressing thoughts or fears and feel compelled to perform rituals such as washing hands repeatedly, checking things, or counting. These compulsions are an attempt to manage the anxiety caused by obsessive thoughts, but they often interfere with daily functioning. According to the International OCD Foundation, about 1 in 100 children suffer from OCD.

Treatment for OCD and Other Anxiety Disorders: Exposure and Response Prevention (ERP), a type of cognitive-behavioral therapy, is highly effective for treating OCD. ERP involves gradually exposing the child to the source of their anxiety while preventing them from engaging in compulsive behaviors. This helps them learn that their fears are manageable and reduces the need for compulsions. Medication, particularly SSRIs, may also be used alongside therapy for severe cases of OCD.

Coping with Anxiety Disorders: For children with anxiety disorders, it's important to establish routines that create a sense of stability and predictability. Encouraging open conversations about their fears and teaching relaxation techniques, such as mindfulness or progressive muscle relaxation, can help them manage their anxiety. Schools and families should collaborate to provide accommodations, such as extended test time or designated "quiet spaces," to reduce stress in academic settings.

Action Plans to Overcome Childhood Disorders

Early Detection and Intervention: Timely diagnosis and early intervention are critical for managing childhood disorders effectively. Regular developmental screenings in schools and pediatric clinics can help identify early signs of autism, ADHD, anxiety, and other disorders, enabling parents and healthcare providers to intervene before the condition worsens.

Multidisciplinary Approach to Treatment: Managing childhood disorders requires a collaborative approach that includes mental health professionals, pediatricians, teachers, and parents. Coordinating care across these fields ensures that the child receives comprehensive support tailored to their needs.

Parent and Caregiver Education: Educating parents and caregivers about childhood disorders equips them with the knowledge and skills to support their children. Parent training programs that focus on behavioral management strategies and emotional support can significantly improve outcomes for children with disorders such as ADHD and anxiety.

Creating Supportive School Environments: Schools play a vital role in supporting children with mental health disorders. Implementing individualized education plans (IEPs) and providing accommodations such as additional time for assignments or a quiet space can help children with disorders thrive academically and socially.

Conclusion

Childhood disorders such as Autism Spectrum Disorder, ADHD, anxiety, depression, and OCD can present significant challenges for children and their families. However, with early detection, appropriate treatment, and a supportive environment, children with these disorders can lead fulfilling lives and reach their full potential. By employing a multidisciplinary approach that involves mental health professionals, educators, and families, and by providing tailored support to meet each child's unique needs, we can ensure that children with these conditions are given the best chance to succeed.

Through awareness, understanding, and proactive management, the emotional and behavioral challenges associated with childhood disorders can be mitigated, allowing children to flourish and develop into emotionally healthy and resilient individuals.

Chapter 17
Child Abuse & Neglect

"Abuse changes your life…Fight Back and change the life of your abusers by breaking your silence on abuse!"
— Patty Rase

Child abuse and neglect are deeply troubling realities that affect millions of children worldwide, and India is no exception. According to a 2007 study by the Ministry of Women and Child Development in India, two out of three children were reported to have experienced physical abuse, and over half faced emotional abuse.

These numbers reflect the widespread nature of abuse and neglect, cutting across all socio-economic backgrounds. Child abuse can take many forms, including physical, emotional, sexual, and neglect, and its impact can have lifelong repercussions on a child's emotional, mental, and physical well-being. This chapter delves into recognizing the signs of abuse, the psychological impact of neglect and abuse, the pressures Indian parents and teachers impose on children, and the importance of support systems and interventions to help children in crisis.

Recognizing the Signs of Abuse

Identifying abuse and neglect in children is a critical step toward intervention and healing. Abuse can manifest in various forms, including physical, emotional, and sexual, and neglect is often seen through signs of unmet basic needs such as food, shelter, and care.

Physical Abuse: Physical abuse involves causing deliberate harm to a child through actions like hitting, shaking, or burning. Signs of physical abuse may include unexplained bruises, burns, cuts, or broken bones. Children who are physically abused may also exhibit fearfulness toward adults or an aversion to being touched.

Emotional Abuse: Emotional abuse, often more difficult to detect, involves behaviors that harm a child's emotional health or sense of self-worth. This includes verbal abuse, constant criticism, humiliation, or rejection. Children who face emotional abuse may exhibit low self-esteem, anxiety, depression, or withdrawal from social interactions. They may also have difficulty forming healthy relationships due to a lack of emotional security.

Sexual Abuse: Sexual abuse involves inappropriate touching, exposure to sexual content, or sexual exploitation of a child. Children who are sexually abused may display sudden changes in behavior, regress to earlier developmental stages (such as bedwetting), show knowledge of sexual topics beyond their age, or develop fear toward certain adults or places.

Neglect: Neglect is the failure to provide for a child's basic physical, emotional, or educational needs. Neglected children may frequently be hungry, inadequately clothed, or left unsupervised for long periods. They may also show signs of poor hygiene, developmental delays, and frequent absenteeism from school.

The Psychological Impact of Neglect and Abuse

The psychological impact of abuse and neglect can be devastating, leaving deep emotional wounds that may last well into adulthood. Children who experience abuse and neglect are at higher risk for developing mental health disorders, difficulties in relationships, and problems with self-esteem.

Trauma and Mental Health: Children who are abused or neglected often experience post-traumatic stress disorder (PTSD), anxiety, depression, and difficulty regulating emotions. The constant state of fear and insecurity caused by abuse disrupts the brain's ability to process emotions and manage stress. Research indicates that children exposed to chronic abuse may suffer from long-term cognitive and emotional impairments, including difficulty concentrating and learning.

Trust and Attachment Issues: Abused children frequently struggle with trust and attachment. Their early experiences with caregivers, who should be their source of protection and support, instead become associated with harm and neglect. This leads to difficulty forming healthy relationships with peers, teachers, and future partners, and often results in social withdrawal or problematic attachment patterns such as clinginess or extreme detachment.

Self-Esteem and Behavioral Issues: Abuse can severely damage a child's self-esteem. Children who are emotionally or physically mistreated often internalize the abuse, believing they are unworthy of love or inherently flawed.

This can result in behavioral issues such as aggression, defiance, or self-harm. Some children may develop perfectionism or overachieving tendencies as a way to gain approval, while others may exhibit withdrawal, avoidance of responsibility, or academic failure.

Support Systems for Children in Crisis

For children who have experienced abuse or neglect, support systems are essential to their recovery. These systems include family, friends, teachers, counselors, and social services that can provide emotional, psychological, and practical support to help the child heal and rebuild their life.

Family and Community Support: For children who have been abused, family support is critical—if the family is not the source of the abuse. Parents or guardians who can provide a safe and nurturing environment can help restore the child's sense of trust and security. Extended family members, neighbors, and community leaders also play an important role in providing emotional support and monitoring the child's well-being.

School-Based Support Systems: Teachers and school counselors are often the first to notice signs of abuse or neglect. Schools should have robust systems in place to provide emotional and academic support for children who have experienced trauma. This includes counseling services, peer support groups, and specialized programs that help children cope with trauma and manage their emotions.

Professional Counseling and Therapy: Professional therapy is a key component in helping children recover from abuse. Trauma-focused cognitive-behavioral therapy (TF-

CBT) is commonly used to treat children who have experienced abuse, as it helps them process the trauma and develop coping strategies. Play therapy is also an effective tool for younger children to express their emotions and rebuild trust.

"Children are resilient, but we must give them the right tools to heal."
— Unknown

Legal and Therapeutic Interventions

Legal and therapeutic interventions are crucial for protecting children from abuse and providing them with the necessary resources for recovery. Legal frameworks in India, such as the Protection of Children from Sexual Offences (POCSO) Act, aim to safeguard children from abuse, while therapeutic interventions focus on healing and emotional recovery.

Legal Protections: India's legal system has taken significant steps to address child abuse. The POCSO Act, 2012, specifically focuses on protecting children from sexual offenses, ensuring that perpetrators are brought to justice. Additionally, the Juvenile Justice (Care and Protection of Children) Act provides guidelines for the protection, care, and rehabilitation of abused children. However, a lack of awareness and societal stigma often results in underreporting of cases.

Child Protective Services and Helplines: Government and non-government organizations in India provide essential services to protect children in crisis. Childline India, for example, is a helpline dedicated to providing immediate assistance to children in distress. Social workers and child protection officers are trained to intervene in cases of abuse, ensure the safety of the child, and provide legal and psychological support.

Therapeutic Interventions: Children who have experienced abuse require long-term therapeutic interventions to help them process their trauma. Therapy can include one-on-one counseling, group therapy, or family therapy, depending on the child's needs. It is important to ensure that children have access to trauma-informed care, which takes into consideration the specific emotional needs of abused children.

Pressure on Indian Parents & Teachers

In India, the pressure placed on children by parents and teachers to succeed academically can also contribute to forms of emotional abuse or neglect. The Indian education system is highly competitive, and many children face immense pressure to excel in exams and secure future success.

Academic Pressure and Mental Health: Indian parents and teachers often have high academic expectations, pushing children to excel in school. While motivation is important, excessive pressure can lead to stress, anxiety, and emotional burnout. In extreme cases, children may suffer from depression or suicidal thoughts due to the overwhelming demands placed on them. According to the National Crime Records Bureau, academic-related stress is one of the leading causes of suicides among adolescents in India.

Emotional Neglect Due to Overemphasis on Success: The focus on academic success often leads to emotional neglect, where children's mental and emotional needs are overlooked in favor of academic achievement. This neglect can cause long-term damage to a child's self-esteem and emotional resilience, leaving them ill-equipped to handle failure or setbacks later in life.

"Children need guidance and sympathy far more than instruction." — Anne Sullivan

Action Plans to Overcome Child Abuse and Neglect

Raise Awareness and Reduce Stigma: Conduct awareness campaigns in schools, communities, and families to educate people about the signs of child abuse and neglect. Reducing societal stigma around reporting abuse is essential to protecting children and preventing further harm.

Strengthen Legal Frameworks and Enforcement: Ensure that existing laws, such as the POCSO Act, are strictly enforced. Police, educators, and social workers should receive training on child protection laws to identify and respond to cases of abuse effectively.

Provide Access to Mental Health Support: Offer mental health services in schools and communities, particularly for children dealing with trauma. Trained counselors and psychologists should be available to provide ongoing support for children who have experienced abuse.

Promote Positive Parenting and Teaching: Encourage parents and teachers to adopt more supportive and empathetic approaches when dealing with children. Workshops on positive parenting and stress management can help reduce the emotional burden placed on children.

Conclusion

Child abuse and neglect are pervasive issues that require urgent attention from all sectors of society. Recognizing the signs of abuse, understanding the long-term psychological impact, and providing children with appropriate support systems are critical steps in addressing this issue. Legal and therapeutic interventions, when combined with increased awareness and societal change, can help protect vulnerable children and promote healing.

As we work toward creating a safer world for children, we must also challenge the pressures and expectations that contribute to emotional neglect, particularly in the Indian context where academic success often overshadows emotional well-being. By ensuring that children are nurtured, protected, and supported, we can empower them to grow into healthy, confident individuals.

Chapter 18
The Role of Play in Child Development

"Play is the highest form of research."
– Albert Einstein

Play is a crucial element in child development, serving as a natural and essential way for children to explore the world, learn new skills, and process emotions. Through play, children develop physically, cognitively, emotionally, and socially. It is not just a leisure activity but a powerful tool for learning and growth. The benefits of play extend beyond childhood and lay the foundation for lifelong social, cognitive, and emotional well-being.

Studies have consistently demonstrated the importance of play in childhood. According to the **American Academy of Pediatrics**, play contributes to healthy brain development and is crucial for building creativity, problem-solving skills, and social competence. In fact, research shows that children who engage in regular, free play perform better academically and develop stronger social skills. The **Centers for Disease Control and Prevention**

(CDC) also emphasizes the importance of play in reducing childhood stress and promoting emotional resilience.

This chapter explores the different types of play, the role of imaginative play in emotional development, how social play fosters friendships, and the therapeutic benefits of play therapy. These aspects demonstrate how play is not only a source of joy but also a key component in shaping a child's emotional and psychological health.

Types of Play and Their Psychological Benefits

"Children learn as they play. Most importantly, in play, children learn how to learn."– O. Fred Donaldson

Play can take many forms, each offering unique psychological benefits that contribute to a child's holistic development. Some of the primary types of play include **physical play**, **constructive play**, **imaginative play**, and **social play**.

Physical Play: Involves activities like running, jumping, and climbing. This type of play helps children develop gross motor skills, coordination, and physical strength. It also promotes cognitive development by teaching children to assess risks and make decisions quickly.

Constructive Play: Involves building or creating things, such as stacking blocks or drawing. This type of play fosters creativity, problem-solving, and fine motor skills. Children learn to manipulate their environment, experiment with different materials, and enhance their ability to focus on tasks.

Imaginative Play: Allows children to create stories and scenarios. Whether they pretend to be superheroes, doctors, or animals, imaginative play is vital for emotional development as it helps children process their feelings and explore different perspectives.

Social Play: Involves interacting with others, learning how to cooperate, share, and navigate social roles. It teaches empathy, negotiation, and conflict resolution, helping children form friendships and build communication skills.

Action Plan:Encourage different types of play by providing children with a variety of toys and materials. Allow them time for free play and create safe environments where they can explore both structured and unstructured play. For physical play, outdoor activities such as playground visits, sports, or nature walks are beneficial.

The Role of Imaginative Play in Emotional Growth

"Play gives children a chance to practice what they are learning."– Fred Rogers

Imaginative play, also known as pretend or make-believe play, is particularly crucial for emotional development. Through imaginative play, children engage in role-playing, which allows them to explore emotions, understand social roles, and develop empathy. This type of play helps children process complex emotions such as fear, anger, and sadness, and express feelings they may not yet have the vocabulary to articulate.

Example 1: A child who plays "doctor" is not only practicing social roles but also processing experiences they may have had during a visit to the doctor. This helps the child gain control over their environment and reduces anxiety associated with real-life medical situations.

Example 2: A child pretending to be a superhero might be expressing a desire for power or control in situations where they feel helpless. This form of play allows them to explore feelings of competence and bravery in a safe, imaginary context.

Example 3: When children create family scenarios during play, such as imitating parental roles or resolving conflicts between dolls, they practice emotional regulation and empathy. They rehearse social interactions and emotions that are central to their relationships with family members and friends.

Action Plan:

Foster imaginative play by providing costumes, props, and storybooks that inspire children to create their own worlds. Encourage children to engage in role-playing games and support their imaginative efforts by participating in their make-believe worlds. Imaginative play can be enhanced through storytelling, puppet shows, or simply allowing children time and space to create their own narratives.

Social Play and the Development of Friendships

"It is a happy talent to know how to play."
— Ralph Waldo Emerson

Social play is essential for developing interpersonal skills and forming friendships. Through social play, children learn how to cooperate, share, take turns, and resolve conflicts. These interactions help children develop emotional intelligence, learn to manage social dynamics, and understand the importance of relationships. Friendships built during social play form the foundation of a child's social network, providing emotional support and a sense of belonging.

Example 1: A group of children playing a team sport, such as soccer, must work together to achieve a common goal. This not only fosters teamwork but also teaches children about fairness, leadership, and how to handle winning or losing gracefully.

Example 2: In a preschool setting, children playing together in a sandbox learn to negotiate roles and responsibilities—one child may build a sandcastle while another fetches water. These cooperative experiences teach children the value of collaboration and how to work toward shared goals.

Example 3: Playdates offer an opportunity for children to interact one-on-one with peers, building strong individual friendships. These interactions often involve problem-solving when disagreements arise, helping children learn to navigate social conflicts and develop emotional resilience.

Statistics: According to a study published in **Pediatrics** (2018), children who engage in regular social play are 34% more likely to develop better conflict-resolution skills and are more likely to form close friendships compared to children who engage in solitary play.

Action Plan: Encourage social play by arranging playdates, enrolling children in team sports, or facilitating group activities like board games or art projects. Teach children the importance of sharing and taking turns during play, and guide them in resolving conflicts constructively when disagreements occur. Create opportunities for cooperative play in both structured and unstructured settings.

Play Therapy: A Tool for Healing

"Play is often talked about as if it were a relief from serious learning. But for children, play is serious learning."– Fred Rogers

Play therapy is a psychological treatment method used to help children express their feelings, process trauma, and work through behavioral issues. It is particularly useful for children who may not have the language skills to articulate their emotions. Through play, children can express what they may not be able to put into words, making it an effective therapeutic tool for addressing anxiety, depression, trauma, and other emotional challenges.

Example 1: A child who has experienced trauma may use dolls or action figures during play therapy to reenact situations they find distressing. This process allows the child to explore their feelings in a safe space and gain a sense of control over their experiences.

Example 2: A child with social anxiety might engage in role-playing games during therapy, where they practice social interactions in a controlled environment. This helps the child build confidence and develop coping strategies for real-life social situations.

Example 3: Children dealing with parental separation or divorce may use sand tray therapy, a type of play therapy where they build scenes using miniature figures and objects in a sand tray. This nonverbal method allows children to express complex emotions related to family dynamics.

Statistics: According to the **Association for Play Therapy (APT)**, play therapy has been shown to be effective in treating emotional and behavioral problems, with over 70% of children showing improvement after play therapy sessions.

Action Plan: For children experiencing emotional or behavioral challenges, consider consulting with a licensed play therapist. Create a supportive environment at home where children feel safe to express their emotions through play. Encourage open communication and be present during play sessions to provide emotional support.

Conclusion

Play is far more than a simple pastime for children—it is a fundamental component of their development. From building motor skills and cognitive abilities to fostering emotional growth and social connections, play shapes the way children interact with the world. Whether it is imaginative play that allows children to process their emotions, social play that helps develop friendships, or therapeutic play used to heal trauma, each form of play has lasting benefits.

As adults, it is essential to recognize the power of play and to create environments that encourage and support it. By offering a variety of play opportunities, engaging with children in their imaginative worlds, and ensuring they have the space to explore their emotions through play, we help lay the groundwork for their future success and well-being.

"Play is the work of childhood."
– Jean Piaget

Chapter 19
Resilience and Coping in Childhood

"Children are not things to be molded, but are people to be unfolded." – Jess Lair

Resilience is the ability to bounce back from challenges, stress, or difficult situations. It helps people adapt positively, stay strong, and keep going even when facing tough times. For children, resilience means learning to manage their emotions, solve problems, and seek support when needed. Building resilience involves support from family, friends, and teachers, helping children grow into confident, adaptable adults who can handle life's ups and downs.

Statistics indicate that childhood adversity is more common than we might think. According to the **Centers for Disease Control and Prevention (CDC),** nearly 60% of adults report experiencing at least one adverse childhood experience (ACE) such as abuse, neglect, or household dysfunction. Despite these challenges, many children are able to thrive due to their resilience and the support systems around them. Fostering emotional resilience early in life provides a protective buffer that enables children to cope with difficulties and maintain their mental health.

In this chapter, we will explore the importance of fostering emotional resilience, coping mechanisms for handling stress and trauma, the role of family support in building resilience, and strategies for helping children cope with grief and loss.

Fostering Emotional Resilience in Children

Emotional resilience allows children to deal with challenges in a healthy manner and helps them develop self-efficacy, emotional regulation, and problem-solving skills. Children who are emotionally resilient are better equipped to manage setbacks, learn from mistakes, and continue striving despite difficulties.Resilience is not an inherent trait; it is built over time through experiences, supportive relationships, and learning how to manage emotions. Key components of fostering resilience include teaching children how to express their emotions appropriately, helping them build a positive self-concept, and encouraging a growth mindset that views challenges as opportunities for learning.

Action Plan:

Encourage problem-solving: Allow children to face challenges and guide them through solving problems independently. For instance, if a child faces difficulty in a group project at school, help them brainstorm solutions rather than stepping in to resolve the issue for them.

Promote emotional awareness: Teach children how to recognize and label their emotions. When children can identify feelings like sadness, anger, or frustration, they are more capable of managing them effectively.

Model resilience: Parents and caregivers should mo del resilience by handling their own stress in healthy ways. Children observe how adults react to difficulties, and these behaviors influence their own coping strategies.

Coping Mechanisms for Stress and Trauma

"In every life, we have some trouble, but when you worry, you make it double." – Bobby McFerrin

Children, like adults, experience stress, and in some cases, trauma. Stress may come from everyday pressures like schoolwork, friendships, or conflicts at home. Trauma, however, can stem from more significant events such as witnessing violence, the loss of a loved one, or experiencing abuse. Developing effective coping mechanisms helps children manage both everyday stress and traumatic experiences without long-term psychological harm.

Common coping mechanisms include emotional expression, physical activity, creative outlets, and seeking comfort from trusted adults. It is important to remember that children need guidance to develop healthy coping skills. Without such guidance, they may adopt maladaptive behaviors like avoidance, aggression, or withdrawal.

Action Plan:

❖ **Encourage open communication**: Create an environment where children feel safe discussing their worries and fears. Regularly check in with children about their feelings and provide them with a non-judgmental space to express themselves.

❖ **Teach relaxation techniques**: Activities like deep breathing, progressive muscle relaxation, and mindfulness can help children calm their nervous system during stressful moments. These techniques can be practiced during times of low stress so that children can use them more effectively when needed.

❖ **Engage in physical activities**: Physical exercise is a well-documented stress reliever. Encourage children to engage in outdoor activities, sports, or simple exercises like dancing or yoga to help them cope with stress.

Research from the **National Child Traumatic Stress Network (NCTSN)** suggests that nearly 30% of children who experience trauma develop post-traumatic stress disorder (PTSD). However, children who receive early intervention and support are significantly less likely to experience long-term emotional difficulties.

The Role of Family Support in Building Resilience

"To nurture a garden is to feed not just the body, but the soul." – Alfred Austin

Family support plays a vital role in building resilience in children. A strong family unit provides children with emotional security, stability, and a sense of belonging, all of which are essential for resilience. Children who feel connected to their families are more likely to have the confidence to tackle challenges and bounce back from adversity.

Parents and caregivers are often the first line of defense when a child faces difficulties. By providing consistent love, support, and encouragement, families help children build the internal resources they need to thrive. Simple acts of providing a listening ear, offering reassurance, and setting clear boundaries contribute to a child's ability to manage stress and recover from setbacks.

Action Plan:

- **Foster open family communication**: Encourage regular family meetings or discussions where everyone is invited to share their thoughts and feelings. This helps children feel heard and understood, which is key for building resilience.
- **Set clear expectations**: Children thrive on structure and knowing what is expected of them. Providing clear rules and boundaries gives them a sense of security and helps them manage their emotions more effectively.
- **Provide emotional support**: During difficult times, ensure that children know they have someone to turn to. Offer comfort, listen to their concerns, and remind them that they are not alone in facing their challenges.

According to the **Harvard Center on the Developing Child**, strong, supportive relationships with family members are the most important factor in building resilience in children. Studies show that children with stable family environments are 40% more likely to recover from adversity compared to those who lack such support.

Strategies for Helping Children Cope with Grief and Loss

"Grief and loss are inevitable parts of life, and children are not immune to these experiences. Whether it's the loss of a pet, the death of a family member, or the separation from a close friend, children can experience grief intensely. However, their capacity to express and process grief is often limited by their age and developmental stage.

Children may respond to grief in various ways, including sadness, anger, confusion, or even withdrawal. It is essential to provide them with the tools to understand and process their grief in a healthy manner. This includes helping them express their feelings, explaining loss in a way they can understand, and providing consistent emotional support during the grieving process.

Action Plan:

- **Be honest and clear**: Use simple, direct language to explain death or loss. Avoid euphemisms that may confuse children, such as saying "gone to sleep" when referring to death. For instance, telling a child, "Grandma passed away and won't be coming back, but we can still remember her in our hearts," helps them understand the finality of death.

- **Encourage emotional expression**: Allow children to express their grief in their own way. Some may want to talk about the person or pet they lost, while others may prefer to draw pictures, write stories, or engage in creative activities as a form of processing.

A study published by the **Journal of the American Academy of Child and Adolescent Psychiatry** found that around 15% of children experience prolonged grief following the death of a loved one. Early intervention, including counseling and family support, can significantly reduce the impact of grief on a child's mental health.

Conclusion Building resilience and teaching coping mechanisms are essential components of a child's healthy emotional development. Resilience allows children to navigate life's challenges with confidence, while effective coping mechanisms help them manage stress, trauma, and grief. Whether it is dealing with everyday stressors or significant traumatic events, the support children receive from their families and communities plays a critical role in shaping their ability to bounce back.

Chapter 20
Conclusion: The Future of Child Psychology

"The way we talk to our children becomes their inner voice." – Peggy O'Mara

Child psychology has come a long way in understanding how children grow, learn, and adapt to their environments. As our understanding of the human brain and behavior evolves, so too does the field of child psychology. With new research, emerging theories, and advanced technology, the future of child psychology is filled with possibilities for even better outcomes in the well-being and development of children.

Children face a rapidly changing world, and psychological support is more crucial than ever. According to the **World Health Organization (WHO)**, 10-20% of children and adolescents worldwide experience mental health disorders, with depression being a leading cause of illness among teenagers. This highlights the importance of ongoing research, early intervention, and societal support in child psychology to ensure that the mental health and overall development of children remain prioritized.

Current Trends in Child Psychology

One of the most significant trends in child psychology today is the increasing focus on mental health. There is growing recognition of the importance of addressing children's emotional and mental well-being alongside their physical and cognitive development. Mental health conditions such as anxiety, depression, and ADHD (Attention Deficit Hyperactivity Disorder) are becoming more widely understood, and the stigma surrounding them is gradually decreasing.

Another trend is the emphasis on **holistic approaches** to child development. Rather than focusing solely on cognitive or academic achievements, child psychologists are advocating for an integrated approach that includes social, emotional, and behavioral aspects. This perspective recognizes that emotional intelligence and social skills are just as important as intellectual growth.

Technology is also shaping the future of child psychology. The use of apps, online therapy, and digital platforms to support children's mental health is on the rise. These tools provide opportunities for remote care, allowing children to receive psychological support even in underserved or rural areas.

Action Plan:

- Advocate for a balanced approach to child development that includes mental health, emotional regulation, and social skills as key components.
- Embrace technological advancements like teletherapy and mental health apps as supplementary tools for therapy and support, particularly for children in hard-to-reach locations.

Emerging Research and Theories

New research continues to reveal critical insights into child development. **Neuroscience** is playing an increasingly significant role in child psychology, offering a deeper understanding of how brain development affects behavior, learning, and emotional regulation. For example, research on neuroplasticity shows that a child's brain is incredibly adaptable, especially in the early years, and that experiences can shape neural pathways in ways that affect long-term outcomes.

Attachment theory, initially developed by John Bowlby and Mary Ainsworth, has been expanded through modern research to explore the long-term effects of early caregiver-child relationships on adult mental health. Secure attachment in infancy is now strongly linked to better emotional health and relationship skills in adulthood.

Moreover, **positive psychology** is gaining traction in child development. This approach emphasizes strengths, well-being, and resilience rather than focusing solely on diagnosing and treating deficits. Positive psychology interventions, such as teaching children gratitude, mindfulness, and kindness, have shown promising results in boosting emotional resilience and mental well-being.

Action Plan:

- Encourage the application of neuroscience in creating educational tools and strategies that cater to individual developmental needs, such as personalized learning plans that reflect a child's cognitive abilities.

The Importance of Early Intervention

"An ounce of prevention is worth a pound of cure."
– Benjamin Franklin

Early intervention is one of the most powerful tools in child psychology. When developmental challenges or mental health issues are identified and addressed early, children are more likely to overcome obstacles and lead healthy, fulfilling lives. The earlier interventions take place, the more adaptable a child's brain is, allowing for better outcomes in behavior, learning, and emotional regulation.

For children with developmental disorders such as **autism**, **ADHD**, or **learning disabilities**, early diagnosis and treatment can significantly improve their quality of life. Early intervention programs that involve speech therapy, occupational therapy, or behavioral interventions are proven to help children develop the skills they need to succeed in school and social environments.

Action Plan:

- Screen for developmental delays and mental health concerns early, ideally during regular pediatric visits, to identify potential issues before they become more pronounced.
- Educate parents and caregivers on the signs of developmental challenges and encourage them to seek help promptly if they notice delays or difficulties.
- Advocate for accessible early intervention services, particularly in low-income or rural areas, where such services may be limited.

The **National Institute of Child Health and Human Development (NICHD)** highlights that early intervention services have led to improved educational outcomes for 70% of children with developmental delays. Furthermore, children receiving intervention before age three are more likely to meet developmental milestones.

How Society Can Support Healthy Childhood Development

"It takes a village to raise a child."– *African Proverb*

Healthy childhood development is not just the responsibility of parents and caregivers but of society as a whole. Communities, schools, healthcare systems, and governments all play critical roles in supporting the growth and well-being of children.

Schools: Education systems are a cornerstone of child development. Schools need to prioritize not just academic achievement but also emotional and social learning. Programs that teach children about empathy, emotional regulation, and communication skills help build resilience and equip them with the tools needed for mental health.

Healthcare Systems: Healthcare providers can support childhood development by integrating mental health services into routine care. Pediatricians, for example, should screen for mental health issues and developmental delays during check-ups, providing referrals to psychologists or therapists when necessary.

Government and Policy: Governments can promote healthy childhood development by ensuring access to early childhood education, healthcare, and mental health services. Policies that protect children from abuse, neglect, and poverty are essential for creating a nurturing environment where all children can thrive.

Community Support: Communities that offer safe environments, access to recreational activities, and support services for families contribute to the overall well-being of children. After-school programs, community centers, and mentorship initiatives provide additional resources for development.

Action Plan:

- Schools should adopt social-emotional learning (SEL) curricula that promote mental health, emotional intelligence, and resilience.
- Advocate for policies that support early childhood education, protect vulnerable children, and ensure access to mental health resources.
- Encourage community involvement through local programs, sports, and mentorship opportunities that promote healthy development in children.

Conclusion :

According to the **Harvard Center on the Developing Child**, children who receive strong support from families, schools, and communities are 40% more likely to achieve positive developmental outcomes. These include higher academic performance, better mental health, and improved social skills. The future of child psychology lies in embracing new research, promoting early intervention, and ensuring that society as a whole is invested in the healthy development of its children. As we continue to uncover the complexities of the developing mind through neuroscience, attachment theory, and positive psychology, the possibilities for improving children's lives grow exponentially.

9 798889 556308 3